T0196684

Annick Nouatin's
AUTOBIOGRAPHY
PART I
A STORY OF COURAGE, STRENGTH, AND SPIRITUALITY

ANNICK NOUATIN

authorHOUSE®

AuthorHouse™
1663 Liberty Drive
Bloomington, IN 47403
www.authorhouse.com
Phone: 1-800-839-8640

Published by AuthorHouse 2/2/2012

ISBN: 978-1-4685-3669-0 (sc)
ISBN: 978-1-4685-3668-3 (hc)
ISBN: 978-1-4685-3667-6 (e)

Library of Congress Control Number: 2011963467

To all the people who have been there during my life: my parents, my brothers, my children, my aunt and uncle from West Africa , Gregg Schroeder, Georges Selvais, Julia Marie Billen, Teresa Hunt, Nancy Sieh, Robert Lajoie, and my sponsors and friends from Alcoholics Anonymous.

CONTENTS

Author's Note

I WOULD LIKE YOU TO walk with me in my journey of strength, courage, and spirituality. I truly hope you'll like what you are about to read.

I have been writing this book with all my heart. It's about the most important periods I went through.

Some of the names in this book have been changed in order to protect the dignity and privacy of all the people who have played a part in my life.

This book is meant to give courage and strength to every one of you, and I wish much love and light for you.

My Early Years in West Africa

My name is Annick Nicole Pascaline Fifatin Nouatin. Annick is a French name that means "grace of God." Nicole is a French name that means "people of victory." Pascaline is also a French name, and in Hebrew, it means "Passover." Fifatin is an African name that means "everything will be fine." Finally, Nouatin is my last name; in the African language, it means "Trees." That is a little history about the different names my parents gave me.

I was born in West Africa in a little city called Porto-Novo in Benin. Benin borders Togo to the west, Nigeria to the East, and Burkina Faso and Niger to the north. The small southern coastline on the Bight of Benin is where a majority of the population is located. Benin covers an area of approximately 110,000 square kilometers (42,000 square miles) and has a population of approximately 8.8 million. Benin is tropical. French is the main language. The capital of Benin is Porto-Novo.

My father was a handsome, intelligent, and tall man. His native country was Benin. He spent his high school years in Senegal, which is close to Benin. He was very dominant and strict, and his weaknesses were alcohol and control—it was his way or no way. I have few good memories of my father.

My mother was beautiful and looked younger than her age. My mother loved to dress up. She was gentle and subservient to my father, because that was the way she was raised. She was very spiritual and prayed a lot, as though she knew something would happen. She had a good heart but was worried all the time.

We were a family of seven children. I was the fourth child. My brothers were Christian, Jean-Claude, Ernest, Marcel, Charles, and Joel. I was my

1

father's little girl, but he didn't know how to treat us. We lived in a little house. Our lives were poor; we were not protected from infection or death because of the poor condition.

What I loved about Benin is the red ground, the warmness, and the happiness of my brothers. Everybody helped each other, even if they didn't know them.

I was a shy girl who needed more than the normal girl. I needed a lot of love, but I don't remember everything from my childhood. I do remember playing with other children sometimes, and I also remember being dressed in a short brown dress.

CHRISTIAN'S DEATH

I REMEMBER THE LOSS OF Christian, my brother. He passed away because of a high fever at the age of six. My memories of him are almost nonexistent, but I still think about him a lot and I still miss his presence. I can still see his face. My family was devastated when he died. I do recall sitting close to his bed when he closed his eyes forever.

I also see vague flashes of my father holding me in his arms and taking me into his bedroom. After that, I see darkness. This darkness has haunted me for many, many years until now. The reason for this is that my brain blocked some memories.

Going to France

WHEN I WAS FIVE YEARS old, my parents decided to immigrate to France. Since Benin became independent from France, there has been an agreement between the African and French governments.

I don't remember if I was excited to come to Paris or not, but we had to go. For us, it was the unknown. At that age, I didn't realized that I was lucky compared to my people from Benin, even though I struggled very much in Paris. Going to Paris was one step along my spiritual journey.

Paris is known for its famous buildings and works of art, its chic fashion scene, and its modern literary, artistic, and intellectual ideals. I lived in the suburbs of Paris for more than twenty-eight years. Unfortunately, I didn't have the chance to visit other cities around it. What I still miss from there is *la baguette et le fromage* (cheese and bread).

When we arrived in Osny, a suburb of Paris, a three-bedroom apartment was waiting for us. The apartment was very nice, and we were on the fifth floor. I wanted my own bedroom, but I had to share it with my two youngest brothers. It was fine at the beginning, but as we grew up each of us wanted our own privacy. I loved that apartment.

I loved the balcony, because it was decorated with many flowers that my mother took care of with a lot of love. But for some reason, I was afraid of heights and didn't spend as much time there as I wanted.

The whole city was nice. We had everything close by (buses, the train station, grocery stores, and so on). My school was about four miles away from home; my brothers' school was a little father.

My father got a job at the prefecture of Cergy from the government. He was an architect, and his office was very close to the house we lived in. He started his job at the new place a week after we arrived in France.

He went by car or bus … I don't remember exactly. He was well respected there because of his quality of work.

My mom stayed home to take care of us. She was very strong. She would yell at each of us because she was very impatient. For a long time, I wondered why she yelled at us like that. Now I understand because I used to be like that—yelling for no reason.

Paris was new for everybody, and we had a transition period that we had to go through. My mother used to sing all the time. It was a way for her to have some joy, because she wasn't really happy.

With time, I became friends with my neighbors from the same building. On the first floor was a family from Morocco. The family on the second floor was from Algeria. The families on the third and fourth floors were from France.

Djamila on the second floor was the same age as me. Somehow, we became close and spent days together having fun and sometimes doing nothing. She became my confidant, because she listened to my stories. My mother was too busy to provide for my real needs, because she was overwhelmed by taking care of everybody.

My brothers made some friends as well, and Jean-Claude went to school to become a certified public accountant. Ernest was very interested in computers, and he wanted to become a programmer. Marcel was interested of becoming a nurse, and he was really good with people. My two youngest brothers were still too young to know what they wanted to do.

My Kindergarten Years

I started kindergarten when I was six years old. I don't have a lot of memories of it, but I remember my mother walking me to school some mornings.

She crocheted a lot and made me some clothes to go to school. The only things I didn't like were the multicolor hats she made for me. I didn't like them and she knew it, but I wore them anyway.

Because I was new and black, I was seen in a strange way. I didn't feel really accepted. One day, I wanted to play with a group of girls, but they wouldn't let me because I was black. They stood all around me singing, "You are black. You are black. You are black." Then tears came to my eyes. I was a lonely and oversensitive girl. When I think of it now, I ask myself how some kids at that age could be so cruel. I guess education comes from our own families. But when we are in a group, we act like everybody else, but we act differently when we are by ourselves unless we aren't followers. Deep inside, I still have the strange feelings of being in this circle and hearing the girls' song.

When my mom came to pick me up from school, I didn't tell her. I don't know why, but I didn't tell her. I kept all negative feelings inside, because I didn't know how to tell her. I also didn't know if she would have understood my feelings, because she was very irritable.

A mother is supposed to listen to her children and try to understand what is going on. A mother has to be in harmony with herself to be able to understand her children. If we don't love ourselves, we can't love anyone. I think that was the case for my mother. The beginning of my relationship with her wasn't as I wanted to be. I wasn't close to her, and when I wanted to get closer like every child would, she would tell me, "Oh, you are bothering me!" or "Leave me alone!"

I cried all the time and even over nothing. Sometimes, I didn't know for what reason I was crying. I think it bothered everybody in my family. I was the only girl, and I didn't have anyone to rely on except my girlfriends. My brothers sometimes yelled at me, saying "What's going on? Why are you crying? Stop it!" And I cried more and more because of the way they talked to me.

At a young age, I felt unloved, scared, and frightened by everything, even when I was with my friends. I felt like no one had some time for me. My mother did what she could; unfortunately, what she could do wasn't enough for us.

Months later, I became friends with other girls and boys from different buildings, including Muriel. Muriel was outgoing, outspoken, full of life, and beautiful. She was a joy to be around, and she had success with .boys Secretly, I felt very jealous of her. I wanted to be like her—white, beautiful, and successful with boys. I was drawn to her. I was trying to get her attention and wanted to be liked. I wanted to be loved by anyone who was nice to me. Muriel teased me a lot about my shyness, and she taught me a lot about boys.

I hung out with a group of girls who, in my point of view, accepted me for who I was. At that time, I was a follower. I didn't have the courage to be myself yet. My parents couldn't or didn't want to see that I was different.

Ernest use to date a girl named Gaby. She was from Germany and very tall. I was impressed with her hair, because it was as beautiful as she was. Ernest was in love with her, but one day they broke up. He was a player, and girls liked him. He was handsome. I remember being in love with his close friend.

Jean-Claude also loved to have fun, and he and Ernest both smoked cigarettes like my father. But my brothers didn't get along very well with each other. There fought a lot, and my mother would separate them.

Things were not very good at home. My parents yelled at each other a lot. My father wanted his way all the time and yelled at us. He came home from work late and drunk most of the time, and my mother had a hard time accepting that.

One day, my father after dinner was angry at Jean-Claude, because he hadn't done something that he was supposed to do.

From his bedroom, my father yelled, "Jean-Claude!"

"Yes, Dad?" Jean-Claude said.

"Come here. Put yourself on your knees."

"Why? What did I do?"

"Put yourself on your knees, I said!"

My brother obeyed him. Then, my father took his belt from buckle and started to beat Jean-Claude.

Jean-Claude cried, "Please, Dad. Please stop!"

My father was all over him. That was the first time I was scared of my father. He was repeating what he had gone through when he was a child, because he was a tyrant. My father didn't like himself, because if he did, he would never have done that to his children. My mother tried to intervene, but he didn't hear her. When my father stopped after a while, Jean Claude was in bad shape, and he was bleeding and crying. Everybody in the house was paralyzed, including my mother. I was terrified and couldn't move from the corner I was in. I was praying to God, "Please make my dad stop what he's doing to us!" Jean-Claude was crying as hard as he could as he went in his bedroom. The next morning he didn't go to school. I don't remember if my mom talked to him after that, but if she did, she must have said, "Please don't get him angry next time. You know how he is!"

My sick father abused his power as a parent. When he was mad at something, he punished us for no reason. Had he experience the same trauma as a child? The alcohol didn't help. Sometimes, my father called his cousin and complained about us; together they would agree on a physical punishment. I don't recall if my mother intervened and stopped him. She was powerless about all of this. I know something for sure: if she didn't obey him, she got hurt too. Sometimes, I saw her with one eye closed in the morning. Then, I knew what had happened. Oh God, how much I wanted her to leave him.

Unfortunately, this situation became routine in my family, where my father beat my brothers and I witnessed all of that, hating him for doing it. What gave him the right to conduct himself like that? Parents were supposed to protect their children not beat them bloody. Our home wasn't safe because of him. He was a tyrant and hurt all of us. I don't have any memories of my parents laughing together or having a moment of tenderness. I don't know why my father was like this. What was his problem?

Other nights, he would come late and drunk. When I was sleeping in my bedroom, he would open the door and take me into his bedroom. My mom would scream at him asking him to put me back in my bed. She would say, "No, no, no. Leave her alone!"

But of course, he didn't listen. I thought my father wouldn't beat me like he did my brothers, but he did. He used his belt as usual. When he finished beating me, I ran to my mother; all she did was comfort me. As usual again, I didn't know why he did this to me.

A while ago, I started to dream about my father molesting me, and the visions were very clear. My father was sexually abusing me. I used to be angry with my mother; I asked myself why she didn't do anything to stop him or leave him. The answer to this question is that she didn't have the courage to be by herself.

At that time, my mother didn't want to do anything to jeopardize her marriage. Her questions were "What will people would say?", "How I am going to survive?", "What about his reputation?", "Will I have enough money to survive?" It was at that time in my life when I started to dream up a different little world, because my reality was frightening and lonely and had no place for love. I prayed and prayed. I dreamed of becoming a professional dancer, because I wanted to free myself from my own world. I had become scared of my life on earth. I dreamed about angels and guides protecting me, because they made me feel good. When I thought about my future, about being a dancer, it made me feel safe and I stopped thinking that I was a terrible little girl. God became my world and my support.

My relationship with my mother became worse as well. She made me feel like I wasn't worth her time. Sometimes she said to me, "You are so stupid. Look at your cousin. She is smarter and prettier than you." She slapped me in the face from time to time, because I talked back, or my brother surprised me doing something that I wasn't supposed to do. When he told my mother, she said, "Just slap her."

I cried and cried and cried. I became used to this treatment, and I went to the corner of my bedroom to ask God, "Why are they doing this to me again?" I got the answer to that question as a big smile on my face, because I became very sensitive to the answers to my prayers.

For an example of normal life in my family, we would go to church on Sunday. I didn't want to go but my mother forced me. When we came back home, lunch was all ready, because she had woken up early in the morning to cook.

My father didn't go to church; he stayed at home reading his newspapers or watching TV or talking on the phone. Soccer was his favorite game to watch with his glass of wine or beer and cigarettes next to him. It was during those moments that we saw him smiling, laughing, making jokes. He became almost like a normal father, because he was at peace with himself. I would go back and forth, looking at him to see if he was well, because I was afraid he would change his mood. My surveillance about him became necessary, because when he was like that, I was also well. Those times were so precious that everybody was behind the TV, and we would make every effort to make him happy. When he was calm, it was a special day for us.

My father was mentally ill. I didn't have any feelings for my father except fear, anger, and resentment. If he hadn't been there, it would have been the same for me anyway.

My mom felt alive. I liked it when she was like that. All I wanted from my mother was for her to be proud and pay more attention to me. She called me to help or to teach me how to sew and cook; I didn't like that too much. One thing I wanted was to be there for her as well, but my fear of not being accepted for who I was made me feel that I couldn't be there for her. But she has made me a good cook, and that is the way I want to remember my mother.

With time, I became stubborn, and I wanted to be the way I wanted to be. That was necessary for me, because I started to develop survival instincts.

Sometimes, my mother would invite family members and friends to have a good time with us. Family members would bring something. My mom forced herself to be alive and smile at that time. In those moments, we saw her smiling and laughing, and she needed it.

My Father's Death

I WILL ALWAYS REMEMBER THE evening my father died. On a Saturday night, my father invited some coworkers home to have a good time, and as usual, alcohol was there—they had brought some beer. So there was a lot of laughing and joking around.

After a while, my parents argued in front of everybody, because my father needed more beer. He wanted to go out to buy some, but my mother wanted to stop him because he was already drunk. He decided to leave the house anyway and asked his coworkers to go with him. We were left by ourselves. The house became very quiet.

At one a.m., my father still wasn't home. My mother was very worried, because he had been drunk when he left the house and it had already been late. In the morning, she made some phone calls to people my father knew. By Sunday afternoon, we still hadn't heard anything from him. It was unusual for him not to come home. To tell you the truth, I wasn't worried because of what he had been doing to us.

After a while, my mother decided to call the police. They asked her some questions about physical details, unusual signs, why he left the house, and why they had argued. The police said they would get back to us when they found something. Each day became a struggle for us; we were all worried, but we were trying to stick to our routine.

Days later, the police called us back, telling us that they had found my father dead in the river at Pontoise. The car was near the river. The police asked my mother to go down to the police station to identify the body. I wanted to go, but she refused to let me. She identified the body as my father. From the day he left the house until the police identify him, he was dead and in the river.

Many speculations were made. My aunt accused my mom of my father's death. People also said that he had been murdered. I wasn't surprised by that statement because of his reputation of being unfair to some people—I mean that he was accused of owing money to some people.

During that time, my school had scheduled a trip to go skiing. I didn't want to go, but my mother forced me because she was so scared of me being there and asking questions about my father. I left everybody not knowing if I would see my father alive again. While I was with my classmates, I didn't think a lot about what had happened to my father. I really enjoyed skiing. To my surprise, I even won a prize. I was proud of myself.

After a week, it was time to go home, and Jean-Claude picked me up at the train station. He was dressed in black. I became worried.

"What's going on?" I asked him. "Why are you dressed like this?"

He didn't say anything to me. I had to wait until we were home. When we opened the door, I saw many people dressed in black. My cousins, uncles, and aunts were all there and even some people I didn't know. I ran toward my mother and asked her, "Why are they all here?"

"Annick, you father passed away," she said.

I was shocked. My legs were shaking. I couldn't say anything, so I ran to my bedroom. I couldn't believe what I had heard. My father wasn't in this world anymore. I didn't know how to feel. Should I cry? Be happy? I didn't know.

I ran to my mom a second time and asked her, "How did he die?"

"He died in an accident."

That was a lie.

Two hours later, we all went to the cemetery. The people my father knew were all there—his coworkers (who respected him), his friends, his sister from Africa, my mother's side of the family, our neighbors. I was surprised how many people had known my father, but they hadn't known my real father.

I never cried about my father's death, and I had a strong feeling that everybody was hiding something from me. It felt strange to me that my father had had a car accident. I know it can happen to anybody, but I couldn't accept that. I can't remember if my brothers were very affected.

At a very young age, my father had traumatized us for the rest of our lives. I was only twelve years old when he passed away.

After the ceremony at the church when everybody was giving us their condolences, we went back home. I have to say that my father's death left us with a mix of emotions: emptiness, release, and a kind of peace in the house with bad and hard memories for us to keep.

My mother was in bad shape. She wasn't working, and she had a lot of worries about how she was going to take care of everybody. I guess she felt scared and lonely at the same time, but she had been delivered from her husband who had beaten her.

The following week, my father's manager called my mother to offer her a job as a secretary. He said, "We can't be at peace without helping you. Out of respect for your husband, we would like to offer you a job in our department."

When she got the news, she felt thankful, and she started a job as a typist for another department. Everybody respected her and welcomed her. It was difficult for my mother to start working, because she had stayed at home for so many years.

I will always admire her courage. Little by little, she was trying to recover from my father's death and she was on her own.

A while after my father's death, everything changed. Months later, my oldest brothers decided to be on their own and found jobs close to their apartment. I believe they were living life so they could find themselves and also be there for their girlfriends. They often came to visit us, especially the oldest, who passed away a while ago. My memories of the dates are not quite accurate, because I started to live only day to day and mostly on my own.

After my father's death, everything became strange and difficult for me, because I wasn't well myself. I also wanted to be there for my youngest brothers, but I couldn't, because I didn't know who I was. I hadn't felt the love that I should have felt since childhood, so how could I be there for others? Plus I was too young to think about anything except boys.

I spent less and less time at home. Occasionally, I would go to a sleepover. As far I can remember, I started to smoke when I was sixteen; I wanted to be like my friends to feel more accepted. Occasionally, I dated boys who were always older than me because of my insecurity. I have always been interested in dating white man until now. I also started to dress in a provocative way, but mostly, I wanted to be seen and heard. I wasn't listening to my mother. I did chores at home, which I didn't like but I had to do.

My father had taken something from me: my self-esteem, my trust in men, and my innocence. He gave me this feeling of guilt and a feeling of helplessness. I acted like I wanted revenge. The love I should have gotten from my parents and siblings I didn't get. I was scared, insecure, and lonely. I acted out in a big and strange way, and I became more stubborn.

I started to have frightening dreams. I woke up sweating. All I wanted to do was sleep and forget about everything. I was depressed. Something wasn't right with me. I don't know if my mother knew it, but I felt like that at an early age. I had always those feelings of not being loved and feelings of loneness. I felt rejected.

I have to admit that my mother wasn't taking care of me the way I wished. When I think about it now, I still feel sadness. She didn't know how to take care of me. She must have had her owns demons just like everybody else in my family.

My Struggles at School

After kindergarten, I went to junior high school. My primary teacher was Mr. Rock. He was short and heavy with a mustache. He wore glasses, and his voice was very loud. I remember he often asked me to come to the board in front of everybody so he could ask me some questions. I was scared of him, because of his figure and voice. When I didn't answer a question correctly, he asked me to join my fingers and hurt me with a ruler He made me cry several times.

I was a loner. Most of the time, I watched my girlfriends from school play games. Mr. Rock gave us homework to do, but I couldn't care less, because as soon as I was home, I went outside to play with Djamila, my friend from my building. I liked her. After I finished playing, I tried to do my homework more seriously because of my low grades.

After I had been at this school for two years without being a successful student, my mother and the teachers decided to put me in an alternative private school for secretaries called Institute Notre Dame. I had to take the bus to get there. My uniform was a blue skirt, a blue sweater, and white socks with black shoes. I felt cute. I became the target of Sister Dominique. I felt she didn't like me, and because of that, I felt the same toward her. My new classmates were nice, though. I used to take the train with my classmates on the way home.

Because of the way I had been raised with an authoritarian tone of voice, I became a rebel against everything. I felt that my mother was there to command me. Unfortunately, I have felt this way even until now.

I was provocative with the way I dressed to make boys attracted to me. I met a man on the train whom I was attracted to. He didn't know how to be himself, because his way was lying to girls asking them to go to Greece to do some modeling. At that time, I thought that my dream would come true, because of my desire to be a star. I was still living in my own world. I wanted to be there as well as be with my mother and brothers, but my imagination took over. I also wanted my mother to let me go, because I really wanted to go to Greece. That man made me feel like someone special, and I wanted to trust him.

When I got home, I told my mother what had happened on the train, and she went crazy. Of course, she didn't want to let me go because of what could happen to me.

"Don't be so naïve. This is a lie," she said. "I would never let you to do that!"

"You say this because you don't care about me," I yelled.

I was really mad at her. At that time, I felt fearless, because I didn't want to think that someone would hurt me again after what had happened with my father. Even my oldest brothers objected to this idea like everyone in the family. I became more and more rebellious against my family, because I wanted them to let me do what I wanted to do. I also wanted to be in Greece.

I have to admit that I wasn't thinking right. In the same week, my mother called one of her cousins to have her help me see the reality, but I didn't want to hear anything. I was already in Greece.

My Abortion

THERE WAS A PERIOD OF my life when my mother wouldn't hear me at all when I wanted to talk about boys and I was going through puberty. I couldn't talk with her, and she never talked to me, even when I had my period.

One weekend, I was supposed to spend the weekend with my cousin, one I was supposed to look like. On Sunday morning, I woke up bleeding. I thought that something wrong was happening to me. My aunt explained to me that it was normal for a girl at my age to have her period, and she gave me what I needed. I still feel sad, not from having my period, but because my mother didn't explain it to me. It is the role of a mother to do that.

When I got back home, my mother acted like nothing had happened. She knew what had happened, because on my way home, my aunt had explained it to her. Still my mother and I never talked about it.

Another afternoon while she was cooking, I went to see her in the kitchen and asked her, "What would happen if I was pregnant?"

"If you are pregnant," she said, "don't come back home."

"Why?"

"I don't want this to happen in my house," she said.

I found this very strange, because she was supposed to tell me things about boys. She was repeating the same behavior from how she had been raised, and once again, I felt rejected and unappreciated. Unfortunately, she didn't know better.

When I was seventeen or eighteen, I was pregnant from a bus driver. I was looking for love and sex at the wrong place with the wrong people; I wasn't in love with that man. I just wanted some attention and love. When I knew that I was pregnant, I immediately remembered what my mom had told me about me being pregnant. The words I recalled were "Don't come back home if you are pregnant." That phrase haunted me. The following weekend I planned to do an abortion without telling anyone, even my family and friends. I decided to go to my friend's house on Friday after school, lying to my mother and saying that I was going to spend the weekend to my friend.

Late in the morning on Saturday, I went to downtown Paris to a center for abortion. I knew what I was doing wasn't the right thing, but I didn't have any other choice because of what my mother had told me, and I didn't want to keep the baby, because I was irresponsible. Many girls there were in the same situation as I was.

The abortion would be done with some pills. The staff explained everything to us, and it didn't hurt. They asked us to get as much sleep as we could.

I can't explain what I was feeling at that time, but one thing I can assure you is that I was scared during the whole process and I didn't want my mother, my family, or even my friends to know. I kept this secret to myself for a long time. It has only been a little while that I have been able to talk about this with my closest friends. Writing about this makes me realize that I have been carrying this feeling of guilt all of my life. I felt the guilt of being pregnant, because I thought I was a bad girl. I felt guilt and shame.

When I got back home, I said, "Hi, Mom!" I didn't wait for her answer, though; I went directly to my bedroom, and I slept for hours. The next morning, she didn't ask me how my weekend was, and I acted like nothing happened. I really felt alone.

My Attempt at Suicide

On Monday, I went to school, but I couldn't listen to the teachers. I was thinking about what I had done to the baby. The reason I hadn't told anybody was that I didn't want to be judged. I thought that it was bad enough as it was, which is not true.

After a while, I went into a deep depression. I wanted my mother's love and attention so much that I didn't know what to do. In my depressed moods, I wanted to sleep for a long time, and I wanted to commit suicide, I wished everyone would leave me alone. I just wanted to sleep and be in my own world again.

My mother was taking some sleeping pills at night. So on Tuesday night, I went to her bedroom and took enough sleeping pills to make me sleep. On Wednesday morning, she came to my bedroom because I wasn't ready for school. I believe she was worried; she tried to wake me up, but I was still sleeping, and she immediately called the ambulance. All I remember until this day is that I woke up at the hospital and my brother who was a nurse was next to me.

"How do you feel?" he asked me. "Why did you do that?"

I couldn't answer him, and I started to cry.

My brother was embarrassed to see me at the hospital, because his coworkers knew I was his sister. I am sure they asked him some questions, like "Why did your sister do this?"

The hospital kept me for another day for evaluation. They wanted to know why I had taken so many pills. They gave me some antidepressants, which I had to take every day, even until now. I was worried about what my mother would say to me. I thought it would be more of a disappointment for her. I thought very negatively about myself. Then when I saw my mother at home, she asked me not to do it again. Inside, I was mad at her for not giving me what I needed, which was love. She didn't understand that my attempt had been a cry for help and didn't know how to give me love, because she didn't love herself enough. We are able to give only what we have received in the past. The love that I was asking for from my mother … she hadn't had it from her family, so it was hard for her to give to her children.

My brothers also suffered because of the missing love in our family. My brothers didn't know what to say or how to act toward me, and I felt lonelier. My parents hadn't taught us how to be warm and helpful to each other, because they had not been that way toward each other.

After my attempt my family acted like nothing had happened. Actually, what would you want to say in that kind of situation? It was one more taboo that we all stayed away from in our family.

For many years after that, I tried to be the good girl that my mother wanted me to be until she passed away from a brain tumor.

My Mother's Death

My mom was working very hard to take care of us. She woke up early to go to work and came back with bags full of food. Sometimes she asked me to wait for her at the bus station to help her carry the bags. She looked very tired and was having health issues.

I tried to be a normal girl and have fun with my friends. At that time, it was important for me to look good. For a long time, I thought I was selfish for wanting to be like a normal girl.

I didn't know that my mother was suffering so much. She came back from work and started cooking and asked me to help her. Usually, I wasn't happy about that because, after school, I wanted to be outside. My homework wasn't done, and of course, my mom complained. When I felt hungry, I would go back home and the house would smell good because of the food.

Most of the time my mom's bedroom door was closed, she didn't like us to be in there, because she was very private. She knew that my brothers and I sometimes took some stuff that she didn't want us to take (like the key to the cabinet from which I would steal some candies or cookies).

Until this day I still remember how my heart would jump when I saw her on her knees, praying. I felt very sad and wanted to talk to her or kneel next to her, but something always stopped me, because I wasn't close to her. The way she was praying worried me, because when I opened the door I could see her sad face. I wondered if she was praying or crying. I couldn't have a normal relationship with her for many reasons that I didn't know at the time.

My mom was very proud of her appearance—she always looked beautiful—but deep inside, she was very hurt. I believe she had been released by my father's death. We never talked about it. Ours was a house of secrets and taboos with no expressions of feelings; we all grew up like that.

Several times, I surprised her massaging her breasts as though something was bothering her. But she didn't tell anyone of her painful physical condition. From my bedroom, I could hear her crying, but I wouldn't approach her and didn't know why. It was very painful to sense, because I didn't know how to talk to her. To my knowledge, my brothers weren't paying much attention to her either. They were living their lives. She didn't talk to us about her feelings and got mad easily.

I will always remember one Sunday afternoon when I went to my friend's house in the city to do my hair. On that day, I left home and said good-bye to my mom. I sensed that she wasn't feeling very well that day, and something told me to stay home with her, but I went to do my hair anyway.

When I arrived at my friend's house, we start doing my hair. Around four o'clock, a thought came to my mind to call home. I wasn't at peace with leaving my mom without making sure that she was okay. I called and my oldest brother picked up the phone and told me that my mom had fallen on the floor and wouldn't wake up.

"Mom is at the hospital," he said. "She fell down!"

I felt paralyzed and imagined the worst. Then I convinced myself that she was okay and that it was not a big deal.

I shared my feelings with the friend who was doing my hair. She even said, "Well, you need to go to see what's wrong!"

I have to say that I needed to hear something like that to make me go back home and see why my mother hadn't woken up that day. I didn't imagine that I would never see her again.

While I was on the way home, I felt very anxious about the situation. When I opened the door to the apartment, silence was the first thing I noticed. Then my brother was there, shaking.

"She is at the hospital," he said.

I immediately called the hospital—I couldn't stop myself—and they said, "No visitors are allowed after seven p.m." I had to wait for the next morning to go see her. Of course I didn't sleep at all that night; I thought a lot about my mom. My thoughts went back and forth from my father to my mother. I imagined the worst: my brothers and I without parents. It was very frightening.

The next morning, I took the train and the bus to see her at the hospital. Crying, I asked the nurse to see my mom. The surgeon came to me and said, "We tried to save her and did everything we could, but it's too late."

I couldn't believe what he was telling me. I asked to see her, and he let me in. She was lying on the bed with a tube in her mouth. When I saw her, I knew that she was already gone. At that moment, I felt paralyzed again, because I just didn't want to believe what he was telling me.

I was yelling and crying to whomever would hear me, mostly to the surgeon.

"Please, please make her live again. She is the only one that I have, and I need her. Please!"

The poor surgeon couldn't do anything. I sat next to Mom for a long time and cried as hard as I could. A feeling of guilt came to me, and I cried from my heart, saying, "Oh God, if I had only known. I should have stayed with her instead of going to do my hair. It's all my fault."

The surgeon came back to me, telling me that we had to think about the funeral. I looked at him, but I really didn't listen. It was the worst day of my life.

On the way back home, I met my neighbor, who asked me, "What's going on? What are you doing here?"

"It's my mom," I said. "She just passed away."

Oh, Annick, I am so sorry to hear that."

I believed him when he said it, but I was expecting more from him, because he was one of my brother's friends.

I went back home desperate, alone, and very sad because I had lost my mom. I carried a feeling of guilt with me for many, many years. Many years later, I realized that it was my destiny to be without my parents, because at the time I had built strength, courage, resentment, guilt, and low self-esteem.

I went back home and slept until the next morning; I didn't even want to talk to anybody.

My brothers and I decided to announce my mother's death to relatives from my father's and mother's sides as well as to her relatives. Then we decided to do the funeral a week later. I remember that my brothers didn't want to get involved in choosing my mom's clothes for the funeral. I was the only girl in the family, so they asked me to do it. I remember bringing the clothes to the one who was responsible for dressing her, and I wanted to make sure she had some earrings as well. Choosing them was very painful, because I felt alone and couldn't really talk to anyone about my feelings, my guilt, and my anger about this sad event. I wanted the funeral to be over as quickly as possible; it was too painful.

My brothers decided to call my mom's brother and his wife after the preparation of the funeral, and we went to pick them up at the airport, two days before the funeral. Everyone we called came for her. Many people presented their condolences to us. I felt empty, as did my brothers.

My family from Africa had a meeting with us and made some arrangements. I was very silent, listening what they were saying. My family from Africa stayed with us for about a week, and my aunt and uncle didn't really approve of the way things had been set up. I do understand now the way they reacted because my mom was my uncle's sister. My oldest brother didn't respect their beliefs and didn't make them feel welcome. My words didn't counting, and I regret it, because since that day, they haven't paid attention. That was also the case for many family members. We didn't know how to be there for others because they hadn't lived what we had gone through.

When my uncle and aunt left the house, everybody went back to the routine. I remember going to my mom's grave every day; it was like I wanted her to forgive me for something that I didn't know about. I promised her I would take care of my brothers, as though it was my responsibility.

"Mom," I said, "I promise you that I will take care of the family and do my best."

Saying this, I wanted most of all for her to know that I wanted her blessing for being the girl that I was. I wanted her to be there in case I needed her.

After my mom's death, I started to pray a lot, it was comforting, and I became calmer. It was like I needed to connect to my little world. I imagined the best for me. I thought that a prince charming would come to save me from this terrible world. I thought a lot about God and angels, and it made me feel safe to be in that world.

While I was cleaning up my mom's bedroom, I put on one side the clothes that I would use and on another the ones I would give to charity. I opened her drawers and found an envelope addressed to her. I opened the envelope. The note inside was from my father. It said, "I can't live this life anymore. I feel depressed and unhappy and am tired of myself and the life I am living. Please take care of the children. Forgive me for my action. Your husband."

It was at that moment that I understood that my father had committed suicide; he had decided to take his life. I sat down to read the letter more carefully. I was shocked, angry, and sad. *How horrible his action was,* I thought, *taking his own life and leaving us like that.* I hated him for everything he had done to us. I kept thinking, *How could a father do this to his family?* It was selfish and seemed too easy. Even now, I keep wondering why someone would do this unless he has a good reason and that reason is only known to him. For some reason, I kept my father's letter to my mom for a long time to make sure that I really understood the way he had died.

I thought it was not brave of him to do it. I didn't know how to feel. It was one more thing that would keep me from loving him. He had done everything to hurt his family—the mental, physical, and sexual abuse we went through because of him. What I didn't realize at that time was that he was alcoholic, depressed, unhappy, and really sick. I didn't know if I was going to be able to forgive him and be okay with men.

I was the only girl in the family, so my brothers expected me to do what my mother had done, and I started to. My brothers were very demanding and expected lunch and dinner to be ready. They did not help me at all and were very hard on me and not very nice. In my mind, I was becoming the slave of the house. I wasn't doing anything except cooking and cleaning. I saw my friends rarely and was not happy about that.

I stopped going to school. I needed to work and earn some money, so my aunt suggested that I take a test at the Ministry of Equipment. I said yes, because I respected her very much and felt she was there to help me.

I got all the necessary books to prepare for the test, but I didn't prepare seriously. More than two hundred participants would take the test, and only few would be selected.

I did a lot of exercises for my test, and finally, the day came when I had to take it. I didn't feel I was ready, but I went anyway. The test took all day. I finished each part on time, except for the grammar and math parts. I thought, *If it's meant to be, I will get it.*

I went home, and I don't remember whether my brothers asked me how it went. At the time, I was expecting some attention from them, but I didn't know it was difficult for them to be loving brothers. Even now, they don't know how to express their love to me. It's also difficult for me to do the same. I remember that I was the only one who was working. At the time, they needed me and I needed them.

A week later, I received a letter from the Ministry of Equipment telling me that I had passed the test but that I was on the waiting list to be able to work. I waited for the result, hoping that something positive would come from it. I was lucky enough to found out that I had been accepted, and I couldn't believe my eyes when I received the letter. I didn't study very hard for the test, I thought. How come I have been accepted? I was so proud of myself that I wanted to tell everyone who would listen. I wanted to believe that my brothers were happy for me, but something wasn't right about the way they responded when I announced the result.

I received the good news in August, and I was supposed to start working on September 1. The night I received the news, I thought it was a help from God. *God took my mother away from me but he gave me something back*, I thought, *something very valuable, something that will help me start my life.* I was a little anxious to start the job.

Little by little, I became very close to God. There wasn't one night when I didn't pray, asking him to be there for me and my brothers. I needed to pray and feel more secure with the help of God, because it was essential for me.

My Struggle with Depression and Alcoholism

I DIDN'T KNOW I HAD an addictive personality. Since childhood, I had been depressed. I don't know if my parents and brothers knew it, but I was. Certainly, something wasn't right. I remembered being very shy and crying a lot for nothing. I was also a loner. I was different from other children; I was in my little world, and my imagination was very strong. I wanted the best for myself—a nice man I could marry and some children. My dream was to marry a white man. I grew up depressed and alone. I thought that I wasn't lucky at all. I was orphaned at age seventeen. Now I understand why I felt scared all the time, and I didn't know how to tell people.

After my mom's death, I was so depressed that I needed a therapist to prescribe some antidepressants for me. The therapist I saw was a woman, and she smoked a lot. I thought she was nice, and I felt like I could talk to her. She prescribed me some antidepressants, and those pills made me feel better.

There was a drinking problem in my family. When I was born, I was of course subject to this addiction. After my mother's death, I started to drink more and more. I drank because I felt sad, alone, depressed, and sometimes suicidal. I was missing so much love from my own family that I drank even more.

Drinking became a daily routine for me, because I felt the need to be with my friends, who also drank heavily. Drinking made me feel like a new person, and I wanted to be seen as someone who knew who she was. Alcohol made me feel more comfortable in my own skin, so I didn't want to tell anyone of this problem I had. Drinking was also a good way for me to escape because it made me realize that I had some control. My self-esteem increased, and alcohol made me more outspoken with men. My drinking life has always been something that I wanted to hide, because I am a woman and because I was ashamed of it.

One day, I woke up with the need and desire to go back to Africa, to my own town. It was a decision that I made at the last minute. I wanted to go to Cote d'Ivoire in Abidjan, where my father's family lived. The same day, I called them; I wanted to know if they would be there in August. They weren't going anywhere, so I organized my trip and planned to be there for about two weeks. My flight was on a Sunday, and I arrived on Monday. They picked me up at the airport.

I made the decision to fly to Abidjan because I wanted to connect with my roots. It was essential for me to be there; I felt that deep in my heart. I didn't know how to speak the African dialect because my parents had never taught us. It had been difficult for my mother to teach us, because she was very impatient and couldn't see herself talking to us in our own dialect. One day, I remembered asking her to talk to us in the dialect, and she said something like, "Don't bother me." I immediately retracted myself, because that answer was very hard to take at my age, I was sixteen. It was difficult for her, because she didn't know how to be there for us.

When I arrived at Abidjan's airport, my family welcomed me. I spent two weeks going back and forth to and from the beach, being with my cousins, eating, sometimes going to the club, and just being with my family. My trip had been planned, but the family didn't plan my stay comfortably, because I had let them know at the last minute, but I was grateful to be there.

MY LIFE AT WORK

I DIDN'T HAVE ANY EXPERIENCE at all being in a work environment when I started my job at the Ministry of Equipment. I started in the computer division as a typist, and I was noticed because I was fast. I got along very well with my coworkers.

The position gave me a good start, because it enabled me to become a secretary in the same division. I worked in a completely different from the others because I was very serious about my work. My coworkers messed around most of the time. At that point, I wanted to be included, but I wasn't because of the way I was. Like I said, I have been always shy, but people thought that I was snob or something like that so they felt like they didn't want to joke too much with me because they didn't feel comfortable with my way of looking at people. Work was a place where I could be with others, though, and it was very nice for me at the time. It became a place where I was noticed by men because of my cuteness. I have to say, I never thought being cute because I was my own worst enemy. Little by little, I started hanging out with my coworkers outside the work place. I wanted to have fun with them, but I wasn't really comfortable because I was shy and had low self-esteem.

When I started my first job I was eighteen or nineteen years old, and I was still living with my brothers. I do remember giving my oldest brothers some money. I don't recall how the bills were paid, but they were. I also remember that I wanted to move out after seven months of being with them. One day, I couldn't take it anymore. I needed and wanted my independence. So I decided to move out and be with myself. It was a very difficult decision for me.

After thinking about it over and over, one day, I contacted a social worker who helped me find an apartment. It wasn't difficult, because I had an income. I didn't tell any of my brothers because I was afraid they would say no, and I didn't want them to stop me. Deep inside, I wanted them to tell me, "No, Annick don't move out. We need you. You are our dear sister!"

My reality was very difficult, because I never heard those words from them. The day I told them that I was going to move out was very difficult, because I thought I was breaking the promise I had made to my mother about taking care of the family. How could I? But when my brothers found out, they didn't express the emotions I wanted them to feel. They didn't help me with my furniture or clothes, and we even argued. I moved out with the help of some friends of mine; I don't remember their names, but I was glad they helped me.

The one-bedroom apartment on the fourth floor that I found with the help of the social worker was very nice. It was about five or six miles away from the family home. The neighbors were nice. I thought, *Now that I have my apartment, I will be able to see anyone I want.* I was free, and I was happy to be by myself.

Things hadn't happened the way I had been hoping with my brothers. I was surprised to find myself missing them a lot, and I felt so guilty for leaving them. Almost every day, I called them, hoping they would asked me to come back. I never heard that from them.

I found myself drinking more and more. I was also thinking the worst about myself. I prayed a lot and asked God to forgive me if I hadn't kept my promise to my mother. Some nights, I had bizarre dreams that I remembered the next day, and those dreams became real one or two days later. I didn't pay too much attention to it, because at that time, it didn't mean anything to me, but I was wrong. Later on, I discovered that I was having premonition dreams.

With time, I drank more and more just to feel better about my childhood. People don't have to drink every day to become alcoholics. If you have an addictive personality, it's at this stage that it becomes difficult. Once I picked up the first drink, sometimes I couldn't stop until I passed out. At that time in my life, I didn't think I was alcoholic, and nobody knew about my addiction, not even my brothers. No one on my mother' or father' sides asked about me. Only one of my aunts from my mother's side knew that I wasn't okay when we finally talked after my divorce.

With my drinking and depression, I still found the strength to go to work. The work I did was mediocre because of my low concentration. I missed many professional opportunities because of my drinking problem and low self-esteem, and I had a hard time keeping my friends. At work, I hung out with the wrong people. I went out with some coworkers, and after the end of the day, we went out to eat somewhere. Later on, we would go to a nightclub, and when we felt tired after a while and wanted to sleep, we would go to someone's house to get some rest, have breakfast early in the morning, and then go to work. It's not necessary for me to tell you that we weren't effective at all when we went back to work. I do remember almost sleeping at my desk, the same as my co-workers. It was a fun time, though, I have to admit.

My professional and private lives were a mess, and the sad thing was that no one was helping me to direct my life. I was by myself for most of my life.

My work place was in downtown Paris, so I took the train for an hour. I took that time to sleep, read, and dream. While waiting for the train, one thing that bothered me was that people would look at me; I didn't like it. I tried to figure out why they were looking at me. I thought it could have been because of the color of my skin or because they found me attractive, sad, or angry or even because they had their own problems. I couldn't figure it out. Now I wonder if it really matters, but for me, it did matter, because I was always conscious about my looks and how I wanted to appear to others.

When I got my first paycheck, I mostly bought some clothes for myself, and that became a bad habit. By shopping, I was trying to replace the emptiness that I felt. This emptiness had started during my childhood and teenage years. I was very happy when I shopped, and that would last for several days. After that, I needed to buy more and more. It was something that I needed to feel good about myself.

After two years at the Ministry of Equipment, I had the opportunity the work at the National Assembly for about two years. I was one of three secretaries working for four assistant deputies. It was a privilege to work there, because it was the Senate. I did some typing and screened calls. I also had the privilege of talking with deputies from different departments. At the beginning, it was very fun and nice, and I felt very good about myself. But my work at the Senate wasn't very appreciated by my department because of my low self-esteem, and after a year, I was asked to work for a very difficult woman. Some days, my drinking took over and I went home, turned on the TV, and drank. In the morning, I felt so bad that I called my work and told them that I was sick. Several months later, I was fired because I wasn't doing my work professionally.

Once again, I had the opportunity of working for another department with a woman who was very fair to me but who didn't want to continue working with me because of my mistakes. At that time, it became the end of me working at the National Assembly. I wasn't proud of myself.

I was still having those strange dreams that I remembered the next day. One night, I was so drunk and alone that I asked God, "Why? Why me? Why can't you help me stop drinking?" I was miserable about my drinking problem. I just wanted to stop drinking and be normal like others. I would promise myself to stop drinking, and then the next day, I would start again. My friend Marc would come over to use his drugs, which I tried as well, and of course, that didn't help with my drinking problem.

In that period of my life, I didn't have contact with my brothers. Everyone was living his own life, and we had grown up like that, like strangers. I hung out with the wrong people, thinking that they cared about me. That wasn't the case at all, though. I was very vulnerable and wanted to please people so they would like me. I hated myself for not being strong enough to say no to alcohol and for not standing up for myself. It was very hard for me and I couldn't analyze every angle of my life. I wasn't thinking clearly. How could I?

I moved out of the apartment close to my brothers to live in another one that was closer to my job. Then, I was working at La Defense. Laurence, my coworker from the National Assembly asked me if I wanted to move into her apartment because she had found somewhere else to live. I thought it was a good opportunity, and I said, "Yes, I would be interested. How much is the rent?"

"It's six hundred dollars," she said.

Two weeks later, I moved into my new apartment. This one was on the first floor, and I didn't like it too much because of the noises I could hear when people came into and left the building. The inside was dark, but I stayed anyways. I had said yes in the first place because I had wanted to keep my promise.

At work, all the offices were new, and I had a very nice office. I was very proud of myself because of my title. I was the secretary director of human resources. Because of my drinking problem that nobody knew about, I was trying to do my best. At that time, I was very skinny; instead of eating properly, I was drinking. I didn't look healthy.

Somehow though, I was even noticed by men. Of course, that boosted my self-esteem. I didn't take them seriously, though, because I was at work. My opinion of men was not good because of the mistrust I had had of my father. At that time, I still wasn't thinking or dreaming about him. My brain had blocked those thoughts, because I couldn't handle the truth.

My Marriage

In May 1987, I was going home after my day at work. I was walking down the street. I didn't know that I was about to meet the man I would marry. His name is Jacques, and he is five years older than me. He was born in the same city as me, and I knew him because our families had known each other. I had met him a long time before, when I had been about fifteen or sixteen, and my mom and I had been invited by his parents. At that time, I didn't have my eye on him, but I thought he was nice.

He was driving by and stopped his car and came to me when I was walking.

"Hey Annick," he said. "How are you? Do you remember me?"

"Not really," I said.

"I met you years ago when you were with your mother at my parents' house."

"Oh yes, I remember now," I said. "How are you?"

"I am fine. What have you been up to?"

We talked for a while and exchanged phone numbers. A week later, he called me to invite me to have a drink somewhere. I didn't want to, so I found an excuse not to.

Ten days later, he called me again to invite me over for his birthday. I was pleased with that invitation. I knew that he found me attractive, but I didn't know if I wanted to date him or not; I mostly didn't want to hurt his feelings. I decided to go to his birthday party.

His one-bedroom apartment was on the second floor. He introduced me to his friends, and his brother was there as well. It was a very nice night. Everybody was having long conversations, and it was a good time to eat African dishes while listening to some music. Everybody enjoyed the night.

It got late, and Jacques drove me back to my apartment. I let him come in, and we laughed and kissed. It was a pleasant time for both of us. I felt like a teenager who didn't know how to react.

A little while later, we started to date. I didn't know myself very well to be able to know what I wanted, though. I have to admit that, little by little, I let him take over me. I was too vulnerable, and I couldn't take care of myself. It was like I wanted to please him because that was how I was with everybody. I wanted to show him only the good side of me. He knew about my parents' deaths, and he was also familiar with my brothers. I didn't tell him about my drinking problem, because at that time, I didn't know I was an alcoholic. I didn't tell him about my depressive nature either, and I was still taking my pills for depression.

I saw Jacques on weekends and occasionally during the week. One day, he stopped at my apartment without letting me know, and I didn't like it. Nobody in my family knew I was dating him.

We saw each other occasionally, and after several months, he asked me to live with him in his apartment. I don't know why, but I accepted. Maybe I accepted because I needed someone who would support and love me. My feelings for him were mixed as I accepted living with him. I had more consideration for him than for myself.

I wasn't able to show him how confident I was, because I wasn't. I was vulnerable and scared, with low self-esteem. I also had many scars from my childhood, because I hadn't healed from all of that; I was only twenty-nine. When you start a relationship with someone, you need to be happy enough with yourself before committing to the partner. No one is responsible for your happiness. That wasn't my case at all; I wasn't happy with myself, and he knew it from the beginning. Jacques noticed my low self-esteem and my vulnerability. Actually, it was hard for me to hide it. I should have taking care of myself before dating someone, because my scars had a big impact in my relationship with him.

After few months, he suggested that we get married and that we shouldn't tell anyone in our family. I was a little shocked about it, and I don't know why I agreed. I was under his influence. He was directing my life, and I was naïve. I hadn't told any of my friends and family that I was dating him, and I think he had done the same. We fixed the date for our marriage, but before that, he offered me an engagement ring. The ring was very nice, but it wasn't the kind of engagement ring I wanted.

One day, I asked him, "Why don't you have your ring?"

"I don't need one," he said.

It wasn't the wedding of my dreams, and we decided to get married with the mayor. Later that year, we would do a ceremony in Africa for our family. For this occasion, I wanted two members of my family to represent me and two people from his side to represent him. Once again, I was shocked when he said, "Let's do this with two of my friends."

I agreed with what he said. Finally, he invited two of his friends.

We got married on August 23, 1987. I was dressed in a dark blue dress with different colors of flowers on it. The expression on my face made me look like I was confused and depressed. I didn't look happy at all.

After the ceremony with the mayor, the four of us went to a nice restaurant. Jacques's friends congratulated us. The lunch was very delicious, and we left the restaurant an hour and half later. I have to admit that the ceremony was very awkward and very brief. None of us felt comfortable at all, except Jacques, who seemed excited and nervous at the same time. We went back to our apartment, and there I was: married and not sure if I had made a good decision.

Then, we decided to let our family and friends know about our marriage. My brothers, my aunt, and my friends were very surprised when I announced that I was married to Jacques. They didn't understand why I had hid it. It was supposed to be a big and happy event. They told me that I had done it too soon. You may think the same thing.

Once I was married to Jacques, he criticized me and my friends; it was like he didn't want me to see them anymore. My friends weren't good enough. Little by little, I didn't see them anymore, even Alain who had been a friend of mine for a long time.

My work had changed again, and I had to take the metro to go to La Defense. From Epinay to La Defense, it took about thirty-five minutes. After my first day of my marriage, my colleagues congratulated me. Yet something bothered me about the marriage. I thought, *I married him too soon. I didn't know him very well.*

I did have some good times with him. We traveled a lot for a while; we went to Italy, Spain, Rome, and different cities in France. We had good times, but day by day, he showed me another side of him that I didn't like at all.

With time, I discovered that he was very controlling. He wanted his way most of the time. He was afraid that I would be influenced by people and told me several times, "Don't listen what people say to you!"

Several months later, we decided to go to our native country to do the African ceremony called "The Dot."

The day we arrived at the airport in Benin, I was very tired; we had just spent eight hours on a flight. It was very humid, and our respective families were there waiting for us.

I greeted one of my aunts.

"Hi, Tantie, how are you?"

"I am fine, honey. How was your trip? You must be tired!"

"Yes, I am," I said.

After some greetings, Jacques and I went to my mother-in-law's house. It was the first time I had met her, and I felt good, though I was a little nervous about it. I wished my mother could have been there. I didn't think about my father or miss him.

We were so tired that we ate and went to bed very early. The next morning, I woke up fresh. We spent the day greeting people in the village, and at the end of the day, we got more rest.

It always brings pleasure and a deep sadness to go back to my native country. I felt privileged to be with my people, because of the connection I have with them. I always cry when I see them. Over there, I feel like a stranger, and they know that I am not from there because of the way I act and my accent. One regret I have is that my parents never taught me the African dialect, except a few words that I learned by myself.

Before I married Jacques in the African way, I wanted to see Jean-Claude. I took my brother-in-law and Jacques to visit him. Jean-Claude was dressed in a way that made me feel like he wasn't taking care of himself. It was the first time I had seen him after my mother's death, and

I started to cry. My tears were from feelings of both sadness and joy at seeing him. We talked about everything and nothing while he showed me where he was living. Jean-Claude had been always in my mind and heart, because after my father's death, he lost his mind. He started avoiding work, and he invited cousins of my mother's and father's sides to stay with him, because he wanted to help them and himself as well. Jean-Claude had a good heart, but our cousins were not as nice as he hoped.

The day of the celebration for Jacques and myself came. The tradition required each of us to be with our respective family. He stayed with his family, and I went to my aunt's house; I should have gone to my mother's. I was dressed in some blue and white fabric that we call "pagnes." My hair had been done up nicely, and I wore gold jewelry. I was very beautiful. Everybody looked at me like I was a treasure. That was the first time felt that way in my life, because it was the first time I was admired by members of my family. Some pictures were taken. I sat in the middle of a room, and people were all around me like I was the trophy of the night. Of course, it was my ceremony.

The same thing was happening for Jacques. Some family members I even didn't know came to give us gifts.

Both sides of the families got together to eat and celebrate. Each side of the family offered up some presents. Jacques's side gave money to my family, and mine offered some liquor, food, and draperies to Jacques's family. That's the tradition in Benin.

Finally, the ceremony ended late in the evening. I went back to my mother-in-law's house, where I found everybody. I didn't know how to feel about the ceremony. All I can say is that it did have an impact on my future with my husband. I never would have thought that I would marry a man from my native country.

A few days later, we needed to go back to Paris. We took the time to say good-bye to everybody, and once again, I felt a deep sadness at leaving my brother and my people.

We arrived in Paris on a Saturday morning. On Monday, we went back to work. I was very tired but glad to see my coworkers again.

I did my best to be a good housewife. It didn't come naturally, but I tried. For many years, I had been on my own with my bottles. Now that

I was married, I drank only occasionally in Jacques's presence, and at that time, I didn't feel the need to drink when he wasn't home. Even though he used to tell me things that hurt my feelings and though he didn't care about saying them to me.

I thought he was an accomplished and confident man, and I envied him for that. I wished to be as confident as he was.

From the beginning, some red flags told me to be careful. I didn't listen to my intuition, because I was scared to confront him and be on my own. I didn't like confrontations, because I wasn't myself most of the time. I was frightened, because he made me feel the same way I had when I was mistreated by my family. We all have a way of repeating the same behavior we have been raised with.

Losing my Child after Six Months of Pregnancy

EVEN WITH ALL OF THIS, we found a way to have a child. Several months after we got back from Africa, we decided to have a baby, and one day, I found out that I was pregnant with my first baby. Automatically, it brought back memories of the abortion I had had when my mother was still alive. I had kept the abortion secret even from Jacques. I hoped that this pregnancy would be fine.

Jacques was very serious and proud, but I didn't know how to feel about it. It was natural for me to have a baby, because it was part of being in a marriage.

As soon as we knew that I was pregnant, we went to see a gynecologist, who prescribed me some vitamins and asked me to see him every two months. The gynecologist was very nice and very competent.

I was still going to work, and it was difficult because of the nausea I felt all day long. I wasn't hungry at all, and I slept a lot. Everything irritated me. I cried about everything.

In the third month of my pregnancy, we went back to see the doctor. Everything was okay. I was worried about my pregnancy, and I couldn't say why. I shared my thoughts with Jacques, who tried to make my worries disappear. My brothers knew I was pregnant, and they were happy for us.

After the end of my fifth month, the gynecologist did a scan to see whether the baby was fine. Unfortunately, the baby wasn't okay. We found out that he was seriously sick. He had spina bifida. The doctor advised us to have an abortion.

"Even if you go through with your pregnancy," he said, "the baby won't survive one year."

We were devastated, and I wondered how this could happen. The doctor explained that it wasn't anybody's fault and that it could have happened to anyone else. It was difficult to accept this explanation. Jacques also had a difficult time dealing with the loss. I wished my mom could be there to support and hold me. I missed her very much.

The doctor asked us to come back to end the pregnancy. I was six months pregnant, and it was my second abortion, so we fixed a date. After the abortion, the doctor asked us if we wanted to see the baby. I decided not to, because it would hurt me more, but Jacques did.

The doctor advised us to have another baby as soon as possible if we wanted another one. I went through a deep depression. Jacques called everyone we knew to tell them what had happened to the baby. It was very sad. All my traumatic experiences in my life made me stronger and stronger, though—this one too. When I wasn't feeling very good about myself, I asked, "Why do I have to go through all of this?"

Little by little, I became closer with my divine God. He was my strength and my support. .

I took some time away from work and Jacques did everything he could to make me feel better, and I know he was deeply hurt. We tried to go through this period as painlessly as possible.

To change our environment, we went to Spain. A few months later, I was pregnant again as the doctor had suggested to us. We went back to see him, because he was competent and very compassionate.

GIVING BIRTH TO FLORIAN

THIS TIME, THE GYNECOLOGIST FOLLOWED me closely for my first real pregnancy; I had to see him every other month. I was feeling better and better. I was also being more careful about this pregnancy. I went to work as usual, and I tried to exercise a little bit. My diet was healthy, and my self-esteem was up and down. I continued to take my anxiety pills.

I had the desire to learn English, and I decided to take some online classes, because Jacques suggested it to me. My wish was to visit America, because it was a country that I wanted to visit and also because Jacques had visited it several times. I don't remember what happened, but I didn't finish the online classes. I guess I wasn't motivated anymore, and Jacques was mad about it. Jacques was still showing me more and more of his true personality.

I was doing fine with my pregnancy, but I had to rest a lot; that was an order from the doctor. The desire to have a second child was scary. I was an adult child myself, and I was struggling to take care of myself.

My marriage changed, because we couldn't come to an understanding on how to communicate with each other and also because of our differences. We had thought that having a child would make things better, but that wasn't true at all.

We already knew it was a boy, so we decided to call the baby Florian. Then after six months of pregnancy, I dilated too early due to the termination of my first pregnancy. The doctor didn't want to take any chances of losing a second baby, so he advised me to stop working and to stay in bed for the rest of my pregnancy. We followed his recommendation, and I had to take a leave of absence for my difficult pregnancy. I wasn't happy staying in bed all the time, but I had to; it did make things more difficult for Jacques, because he was working. I have to admit, I did enjoy being served in bed.

I got some visits from friends and family. My mother-in-law came from West Africa to help us. She stayed with us for about five months. I thought five months was a lot, but actually it went fast. She was very helpful, and it was a time for her and me to get closer. She also taught me things I didn't know in regard to having a baby. Somehow, I started to consider her as my second mother.

With time, I got bigger and bigger. All I did was eat, watch TV, and sleep. When the end of my pregnancy got close, I had contractions more frequently. In September, I started to have very strong contractions, and because of that, we decided to go to the hospital. I will always remember how, on the way over there, Jacques did his best to get to the hospital, but he had to stop at the red lights, and I couldn't figure out why he was stopping.

"Go, go, go," I said. "You don't need to stop at the red light. The contractions are very painful!"

"Well, Annick, I still have to stop, you know," he said.

When we arrived at the hospital, the doctor was there, and they got me ready to have my baby.

On September 14, 1994, Florian was born. He was six pounds and fourteen ounces. Jacques was in the delivery room, and he became as emotional as me. They put Florian immediately on my chest for me to feed him. He was a healthy baby boy. I cried some tears of joy; he was beautiful. The nurses took him back, and a while later, I breastfed him more. The experience was all new to me. It felt strange and wonderful at the same time. The most important thing was to have a healthy baby boy, and Florian was very healthy.

Two days later, I went back home with Florian. I was tired but fine. My mother-in-law welcomed us home, and I was glad to see her.

I was supposed to start work about two months after having Florian. We were still living in the one-bedroom apartment in a suburb of Paris. Weeks later, we decided to buy a house where we would be more comfortable. I was excited about this idea. The new two-story house we moved into had three bedrooms. We met the neighbors, and I became close with some of them.

Florian was a very healthy, cute, and joyful baby. My mother-in-law helped us a lot. With time, I got back to my normal weight because I was careful with my diet. Many times, I was thanked God for giving me a healthy baby.

As a mother, I didn't know how to really feel. I really wanted to be a good mother for my children, but there is no school for good parenting. I took my role as a mother very seriously, because Florian was my flesh and blood. I wanted to protect him, take care of him, and love him. I wanted to give him the love that I hadn't had when I was a child, but would I be able to do it? You can only provide love when you love yourself; I was very conscious about that. I didn't love myself enough, but I was doing my best to take good care of Florian, because he was my baby.

Jacques and I weren't communicating at all. I was avoiding him a lot. I had some difficulties being a wife for him, and he knew it. We argued a lot. Sometimes, I wanted to escape my responsibilities and everybody. I just wanted people to leave me alone. I dreamed a lot and did not always focus on my responsibilities. I was an adult child. Jacques didn't know how I felt, because I never talked to him about my emotions. It was really hard for me to open myself up to him or to anyone else. I was afraid of being judged, because what I thought about myself wasn't good. It was difficult to analyze my emotions, and my feelings scared me.

After five months, it was time for my mother-in-law to go back to West Africa. I felt a little sad about it, because I liked her, and I was used to her presence. We talked a lot like mother and daughter, even if she wasn't my mother. She talked to me about her experiences in life with wisdom.

With time, I became very comfortable in the house we were in. I enjoyed staying home, because when I was by myself, I felt more secure. I didn't have to pretend that I was someone I was not. But soon it was time for me to go back to work, and I was anxious about it. It wasn't an option for me to not work. To be prepared for this after my mother-in-law left, we hired a babysitter. Her name was Amadou, and she was also from Africa.

I felt very comfortable with her. She took good care of Florian when I wasn't home.

On my first day at work after my baby, I felt very welcome. It was good to see my coworkers again. They gave me back the same position, but the first days were difficult. I saw new faces that I hadn't know before.

Giving Birth to Vincent

FLORIAN WAS TWO AND HALF years old when we decided to have another child. We thought it wasn't healthy for him to be the only child.

I became pregnant with my second child in 1996. At the beginning, I felt the same symptoms as I had in my first pregnancy. We went to see the same doctor again. He really welcomed us, and with his advice, I started to take the same vitamins I had taken when I was pregnant with Florian. He recommended a lot of rest again, and after four months, he asked me to stay in bed again. That was not good for my career, but I had to follow his recommendations.

I spent a lot of time with Florian, and he knew I was expecting another baby boy when he touched my belly. Florian smiled all the time. He was so cute, and those big eyes could kill you.

The new baby moved a lot inside me. At first I was worried, but I got used to it with time. I felt very tired, just like I had with my first pregnancy.

Jacques and I were arguing a lot at the time, and it wasn't good for the baby. I felt very unhappy, and I was crying a lot. He wasn't paying attention to me. I thought deep inside that he knew our marriage wouldn't work, and I felt the same way, but we kept having babies. It wasn't very healthy and was almost insane. I didn't realize it would have an impact for my children. I wanted mostly to make him happy. I was still trying to be a good wife, but I wasn't good enough for him.

My pregnancy with my second child wasn't easy. I was afraid to give him my negative feelings, because Jacques and I weren't doing well as a couple. Sometimes, I needed to escape from the house, and for that I took walks with Florian and the babysitter or just by myself. The last months of my pregnancy were very difficult, and I was worried. I had to stay in bed as ordered by my doctor. We knew the sex of the baby, and we decided to name him Vincent. I really liked the names Florian and Vincent.

The day I gave birth to my second child, I felt some very strong contractions. We went to the same hospital to the same doctor who had helped with Florian's birth. When I held Vincent for the first time, a strange feeling took me. I told myself, "Now I am the mother of two children." I felt overwhelmed.

Vincent was five pounds and thirteen ounces. Again, I had a healthy baby. Thank God. I breastfed Vincent as well. I went home with Vincent two days after he was born.

It was fascinating to see Florian meet Vincent for the first time. Florian didn't know how to feel toward Vincent, and I wondering if there would be jealousy or curiosity, but I was very pleased to see them together. They were two brothers, and I wanted the best for them. *We* wanted the best for them. As time went by, I already began detecting differences in their personalities.

Having two boys was very overwhelming. Jacques and I were responsible for the boys, which was a big thing for me. I had become a mother, and I didn't know how to be a mother. I had to learn. I surely wanted to do better than my mother had by showing some love to my boys. I understand now that my mom did her best to raise us. Still you can only provide what you have been provided by your parents.

During my two pregnancies, I stopped drinking. It was out of the question for me to have any drinks. Jacques knew that I liked to drink, but he had no idea that I was an alcoholic; at that time, neither did I. I didn't have any difficulty not drinking during my pregnancies, and I didn't miss it or even think about it. After my pregnancies, there were a few times when I did have to drink one or two glasses of wine. I was ashamed of this drinking problem, especially as a woman. It was one more thing that I hated about myself. Myself, always myself. I was so self-centered and introverted that I didn't pay attention to anything around me. I wanted to be so perfect that I didn't know where to start. I hid my real self—whom I didn't know—from others. I was trying to show others someone I wasn't.

For a long time, I was angry with my parents, especially my mother. I was angry at her for not taking care of my emotional needs and for being so controlling and authoritarian with me. My father was inexistent to me at the time, and I didn't want to remember him. I was also angry with my brothers for not letting me know that they were thinking of me. I was angry with myself for not being the person I wanted to be. I was an angry, anxious, alcoholic, unsatisfied person. I kept thinking, *Why is life so hard for me? Why have the people I needed the most in my life abandoned me? Why do I feel so different from others? Why do I have some strange dreams?* I wanted some answers to my questions.

Meanwhile, the boys got bigger and bigger. They were very healthy and happy. I was also happy when I was around them. They became my joys, my security, and my life.

My Recovery and Evolution to Spirituality in Chicago

In July of 1998, Jacques came back from work, announcing that he had being promoted for a position in the United States, in Chicago.

"I received a promotion," he said. "My new position will be in Chicago if we accept it!"

"That's great. Chicago!"

"Yes, but I don't know if am going to accept it."

"Maybe we can think about it. It's a good opportunity."

"You have to realize that we would leave everything here—job, friends, family, home—and start a new life over there. How about if we don't like it?"

He was right. We had to think about all angles of the situation. I was so excited about and scared by this news. I have been always fascinated with the States. To me, at that time, it was a country of the good life, opportunities, and success. I always watched every movie on TV. I was also fascinated by the language. When I was in school, I had taken English as a second language. I had been good at it, but I hadn't practiced on a daily basis.

Maybe this opportunity would be a new beginning with new friends, a new home, and a new work environment. Deep inside, I wanted to go, but I was frightened about leaving everything behind. I wanted to change the environment I was living in. I wanted some excitement in my life. When I think about it now, I know that I was already an adventurous person; I liked to take risks and challenge myself. A part of me has a very strong will, and I didn't know it at the time.

Jacques and I had to think about it seriously. We didn't reject the offer, but we needed some time to think about it. We had to think about the kids. Where would they go to school? Where would we live? We had to make plans. Jacques already knew the States, because he had been there several times. Two of his brothers lived there, and before we got married, had he visited them sometimes. For him, it would be less difficult, because he already knew English.

Several days passed, and we made the decision to take the opportunity. We decided to go to Chicago. He made me understand that going there would not be easy, that we would face some challenges. I was okay with it, because I wanted a change. I just wanted to experience one of my dreams.

"You have to realize," Jacques told me, "you won't be working but taking care of the children."

Without knowing what to expect, I said, "That's fine!" with a big smile on my face. I didn't know what I was talking about.

The next step for us was to figure out where we would stay once we were in Chicago as well as where the boys would go to school, etc. Jacques's company took care of everything, and they found us an apartment in a suburb of Chicago called Schaumburg.

My mother-in-law came to Paris from Africa to help us pack everything. It was good to have her back with us. We had so many things to deal with before going to Chicago. We announced the news to our friends and family. In general, they said it was very courageous of us to move to another country and leave everything behind us. I thought the same; not everybody would have done the same thing for fear of the unknown. I had lived in Paris for over twenty-eight years.

Before going to Chicago, I took some English classes with a small group of students. It was very helpful and useful. I wasn't fluent yet, but it would help me.

The second step was to figure out what we were going to do with the house and furniture. Jacques put some ads in the local newspapers to sell our furniture. Friends and family stopped by to buy what they were interested in. Most of the furniture was brought by Jacques's family. We also found a buyer for the house; that wasn't difficult, because it was in really good condition.

It would have been difficult to do all of this without the help of my mother-in-law, who was also taking care of the children.

The most difficult thing for me was saying good-bye to my coworkers, friends, and neighbors. Suddenly, I realized that I might not see them anymore. I felt really sad about it and cried.

Before the move to Chicago, I thought about having a party at my office for the occasion. My coworkers told me that I was strong and courageous to do this; they even envied me a little bit. I decided to have the party on the last day of the week, one week before moving to Chicago.

The closer we got to the move to Chicago, the more everyone was stressed. I had known it wouldn't be easy. The house became a mess, and we had to sleep on the floor, though the children didn't. It was very stressful. I wasn't even sure if I wanted to move anymore, because of the way things were.

Jacques and I didn't get closer at all; we got on each other's nerves. He expected something from me that I couldn't give because of my low self-esteem. For a long time, I thought that, if my marriage wasn't working, it was because of me. That was what he told me, and I believed him.

Our marriage wasn't getting better at all, and I had the urge to drink. I wanted some release from all of the stress, so I sometimes drank while hiding myself. I had thought that the move to Chicago would change our marriage, but I was wrong. Little by little, I went through hell. I couldn't think about leaving him; how could I now that I had two children? I should have thought about it before, when I had decided to get involved with him. We had more bad times than good times.

The day I had my party at work, Jacques didn't come. It was a Friday, and I was dressed correctly and looked beautiful. Deep inside, I was scared, but I was trying to fake it. I wanted my coworkers to see me happy to move on to the next level of my life. The party started at noon. Everybody I expected was there, even my manager. Other coworkers from different divisions came as well. I have to say I was well respected and appreciated at my office. They brought me some beautiful flowers, a book in which everyone wrote a special note to me, and some money that I hadn't expected. I cried when the party was over. It was then that I realized what a big step in my life I was taking.

My emotions would have been different if my marriage was working. I knew my marriage wasn't working, but I still moved forward with Jacques like things were okay. My fears of the truth paralyzed me. My parents weren't happy together; did that mean that I had to be unhappy as well?

The day we would fly to Chicago was coming slowly. Three days before, my brothers came to see us to say good-bye. It was very moving. Our friends stopped by as well, as did my neighbors. When the day we had to go to the airport arrived, I felt very nervous.

We took only five pieces of luggage. My mother-in-law came with us to the airport. Jacques held Florian, and I held Vincent. We met Jacques's cousins at the airport. When it was almost time to get on the plane, we kissed everybody one more time. It was too late to go back to where I had come from.

A new life for my family and me was starting. I was going on a new journey. I didn't know that, little by little, I would find love for myself along with courage and strength.

Finally, we were on the plane. A long flight was waiting for us, which was difficult for the children because of the space. Jacques still held Florian, and I had Vincent. They gave us lunch and dinner. The boys slept most of the time. Jacques and I tried to enjoy some movies. The flight attendant was very nice and helpful. I didn't get that much sleep on the plane; I was mostly thinking about how it would be in Chicago. I couldn't believe it—I was going to America. I am sure that Jacques had a lot on his mind as well.

Jacques showed me some strength, like he knew what to expect in Chicago. At least that was the impression he gave me. We didn't talk a lot to each other during the flight, because we were avoiding arguments, and I hadn't told him about my fear of the unknown or even my state of mind.

After we had been flying for about eight hours, we arrived at the O'Hare airport in Chicago. We had to go through customs, where they checked our passports. After an hour and a half, we got all our luggage. The boys were crying a lot, because they were tired and hungry.

We arrived in Chicago in September 1998. I was in a country where I heard about so many different things, ideas, resentments, different political points of view, and different religious beliefs. I was in a country where racism existed and still exists. It was a nation of different ethnicities. I didn't know how I was going to react to this different culture. I was sure that my experiences in Chicago would teach me valuable things.

At the O'Hare airport, the first things I noticed were the vibrant lights in multiple colors. Those lights gave me the feeling of being a star. I was fascinated by the limousines, which were the nicest cars I had ever seen in my life. After we had been in that atmosphere for a while, a taxi stopped to take us to our apartment at International Village in Schaumburg.

We finally arrived at the apartment that Jacques's office in Paris had found for us. It was a big complex with more than twenty different buildings with different names. Each building had a country name, and ours was called Zurich. We were in a two-bedroom apartment on the second floor with a view of the playground. I thought it would be nice for the children. The kitchen and the living room were comfortable and well decorated. The laundry machines were in the hallway. Little by little, we made ourselves comfortable. It was already early in the evening, and we were all tired, so I fed the boys, and they went to bed.

Jacques and I discussed where we would sign the boys up for school. He told me that, because of the job, he had to go out of the state to Detroit. That news didn't please me. It meant that I would be by myself with the boys for I didn't know how long. I was so tired, worried, and frightened that I went to bed.

The next morning, which was Sunday, we decided to take the car and drive around downtown Chicago—the beautiful country where I wanted to be. I discovered some very nice areas and some less nice areas. I have to say that I was a little disappointed by the architecture of the city. It wasn't like I had seen on TV, but it was a small part of the state, so I couldn't pass any judgment. We stopped to eat somewhere, and Jacques did the talking to people, because my English wasn't good at that time, and he was good at it.

The car we drove was big, old Mercury from 1996, and to get my American driver's license, I had to take some driving lessons. The first time

I took the test, I didn't pass; I had to take more lessons to get take the test a second time, and I also had to become familiar with an automatic car. It was difficult, because I couldn't completely understand what the teacher was telling me, and he had difficulty understanding me because of my French accent. It was really a challenge.

The following Monday, we looked for a school for the boys. We chose a Montessori school with different ethnicities. The owner of the school was a very nice lady who gave us a tour.

In time, the boys did fine. It was nice for them to be in Chicago at a young age, because they could learn very fast. For an adult, it's more difficult. I was so proud of my boys. They looked very much alike, and people asked me if they were twins. I spent a lot of time at the playground where I sympathized with others from different background and ethnicities. That was also helpful to practice my English.

Jacques and I weren't talking to each other a lot. It was very frustrating, because I didn't know what he was thinking, except that he was preoccupied with his work. We agreed that, when the boys went to school, I would also go myself to learn English better. It was necessary for me to be able to have a normal life, and I had to do the maximum to feel comfortable in Chicago.

Two weeks after the move, we took the boys to their first day of school. We were anxious about leaving them with people we didn't know, and I really wanted to feel like they would be okay. At their age, they were not talking a lot, and they knew only a little bit of French. We kissed them good-bye.

On the way back home, I was still worried. Jacques tried to reassure me. The same day, when it was time for me to go to school, he dropped me off at Harper College in Palatine.

Going to School

My first day of school was difficult. I took a class called English as a Second Language, which included some grammar and vocabulary. I also took some math and reading classes. When the teacher talked, I couldn't understand anything, so I listened to what other students said. At the beginning, I expressed myself a lot in gestures because of my limited knowledge of English. Little by little with time, I understood more words. I thought that Americans talked very fast, for me anyway.

After my first class, I was very glad to go home. I didn't have any homework to do. Jacques came to pick me up, and it was also time to pick up the boys. I was so glad to see them, and we all went back home. I cooked dinner, and afterward, I did some chores while the boys played together. After nine p.m., we all went to bed except Jacques.

On Thursday morning, he left for Detroit for work, and I was by myself with the boys. I didn't feel secure; something was missing. I found that I was tied to a routine, and I felt scared. I wanted to drink, but I rejected the thought; it wasn't an option for me. At the time, I didn't know that I was suffering depression from leaving Paris. I didn't know anybody, and the language barrier wasn't helping at all. I wanted to go back to France with my children, but that wasn't an option either. When I wanted to watch TV, I couldn't understand what I heard. I needed a friend to talk to or someone who would understand me. I wanted to talk to someone who wouldn't judge me because of my drinking problem.

Friday went very fast, because my children and I went back to school. I was happy to see my teacher Diane and everybody else again. When class was over, I picked up the boys. My driving wasn't very good, because

I wasn't used to driving even when I was in Paris—public transportation was easier.

Jacques came back from Detroit for the weekend, and we spend it talking about different things. The following Monday, he went back to Detroit for work.

At about four p.m. that same day, I was on my way to pick the boys up from school, and when I got out of the car, I accidentally lost the car keys in the snow. I remember it so well. *Great,* I thought. There I was looking for my car keys, and I couldn't find them. I asked for help from the director of the school, so there were two of us looking for them. A tall man with a hat came toward us.

"Oh, Georges," the director of the school said, "you come at the right time. Could you help this young lady to find her car keys? She lost them."

"Oh, of course," he said

"Hi, Georges," I said. "How are you? Thank you for helping me."

"No problem. I just hope we find your keys!"

We spent about thirty minutes looking for my keys, and we couldn't find them. Georges was there to pick up his two children, Christophe and Danielle. Georges Selvais was from Belgium, and he spoke French as well. He had been in Chicago for more than twenty-five years. Someone was speaking French to me—things couldn't have been better. We conversed in French the whole time. I couldn't believe we had met. At that moment, something told me that it wasn't a coincidence.

After a while, I felt very nervous, because we hadn't found the keys and I didn't know how I was going to drive home with my children. I didn't have a cell phone yet, only the home phone and I couldn't call Jacques because I didn't have his number in Detroit.

After a while, Georges went to pick up his children. When he came back, he asked me if it would be helpful if he drove us to my apartment. I was so grateful, and we gave up on finding the keys, because it was almost impossible for us to find them in the dark. I hoped the car was well parked in front of the school. On the way back home, Georges asked me some questions about myself and why we had come to the States. I found him very nice and polite. The children sat in the back of the van talking to each other. Georges' children didn't speak French very well, but it was nice, because the four of them were having a good time speaking French and English back and forth.

"So Annick," Georges asked me, "how are you going to drive the children if you don't have your car keys and knowing that your husband isn't here?"

"I don't know yet," I said.

"Okay," he said, "I can help you by picking up the children in the morning. At the end of the day, I will drop them off at your apartment until your husband comes back."

"Oh, I don't want to be a burden for you."

"It's nothing really," he said. "I am happy to help you."

I didn't know what to say except to thank him. I was amazed by his generosity. When we got to the apartment, I asked Georges to come in, and we talked for a while.

"Okay, it's time for me to go home," he said finally. "I will pick up the boys at seven a.m. tomorrow. Is that okay?"

"Georges, I really don't know how to thank you," I said.

Georges picked up and dropped off the boys for four days. I was embarrassed and grateful at the same time. When Jacques had called home, I had explained the situation to him. He had said that he didn't have duplicate keys, but that wasn't true. In fact, he had duplicate keys in his closet. I couldn't understand why he wouldn't tell me where the keys were when he saw me and the boys in such a difficult situation. I was really mad at him for several days. Our marriage wasn't getting better. After four days, he finally came back home, and I asked him again about the keys, but he didn't give me any answers.

In the meantime, I was thinking about how I could thank Georges for what he had done to help me. Jacques and I decided to invite Georges's family for lunch on Sunday.

"Georges," I said when I called. "Hi, this is Annick. How are you?"

"Fine, Annick, and yourself?"

"What are you doing Sunday?"

"Nothing special," he said. "Why?"

"I want to invite you and your family for dinner."

"Oh, that would be great. What time would be convenient for you?"

Sunday came, and Georges, Julia, Christophe, and Danielle came over. *What a nice family,* I thought. We had a good time all together, and the food was great. Deep in my heart, I knew we would be friends for a long, long time. Jacques got along very well with them, and the children had so much fun. I was very pleased.

As the evening came to an end, they invited us for dinner the following weekend. I have to say that I looked forward to it. When they left, the house was really empty.

With time, we became very close friends and were involved in our each other's daily lives. Georges and Julia were cofounders of WarmlyYours Company, which they had built many years before.

Jacques went back to Detroit for work the next morning. My desire to drink became stronger. The following day, I couldn't resist anymore, and I bought some alcohol. I didn't drink during the day when Jacques went to Detroit, because I had to drive the boys to school. Usually, though, I drank at night when Jacques wasn't there and the boys were in bed. I drank until I passed out. I hid the alcohol in the kitchen in a safe place; I was always afraid that Jacques would find it. Some days after dropping the children at school, I stopped at a liquor store to buy more alcohol.

I felt so lonely and had no one to talk to about it. I also felt ashamed. My boys were too young to know anything about my problem. I was so confused that I didn't know if I regretted coming to Chicago or not. I was too confused to think logically. I drank because I wanted to forget my difficult life, my past, my pain, my loneliness, my sadness, and my low self-esteem. I drank to escape my reality and to make me feel better. I used to do it because I was predisposed to it; it was already in my dysfunctional family. It was also my nature to live in a fantasy world in which I wanted everything to be perfect. I also wanted to believe that I was perfect. I was a dreamer, because my reality was too hard to handle.

It became a habit for me to drink when Jacques wasn't there, until one day he came home in the middle of the night without letting me know he was coming. That night, I hadn't drunk, but I was scared he would find out where the bottles were. Actually, I believe he knew, but he didn't tell me anything. After he had had his dinner, he went to bed. I immediately took the time to hide the bottles in other places. I thought, *I can't do this for too long. I am sick and tired of hiding myself. I have to stop drinking.* I still didn't think that I was an alcoholic.

Two weeks later, Jacques stopped going to Detroit for work. Then, he was working in Schaumburg, which made my drinking more difficult. Eventually, he found the bottles in the kitchen where I had hid them the second time. He brought them to me, and while looking at me in the eyes, said, "What is this? You have a problem." He was so calm when he spoke to me that I was surprised. I didn't take him seriously, and I didn't say anything.

After all, the children were doing fine. They were growing up healthy. Florian was very protective of Vincent. At school, they were getting along with other children. Their English was getting better and better—better than mine. We spoke French at home, because we wanted them to be bilingual or even trilingual. Both of my children had and still have my big eyes. Florian looks more than me, and Vincent looks like his father.

My English was getting just a little bit better. It was hard for others to understand me because of my strong French accent. One thing I noticed was that Americans love the French accent; in general, people were intrigued by it.

Sometimes, family and friends called us from France. I was even surprised to get a call from my brothers. They promised to visit us.

Georges and Julia became part of our family. We did a lot of things together—going to movies, eating out at restaurants, and so on. Our children played a lot together, which gave us the opportunity to see each other. Georges and Julia noticed what was going on in our marriage and vice versa, but we respected each other's private lives.

Jean-Claude's Death

I WASN'T IN CONTACT WITH my brothers much, and I felt sad about it. One episode I do remember about my brother Jean-Claude was that my mother had asked my aunt from West Africa to take care of him for reasons that I didn't know at that time. Jean-Claude was mentally sick, and he was also drinking. He was working for a company as an analyst programmer close to downtown Paris. It all started after my father's death; little by little, Jean-Claude wasn't paying attention to anything about his life.

One day, Jean-Claude had left his job and disappeared. Nobody had seen him, even the family living with him. My mother called the police. We prayed a lot to find him. On a Sunday, a priest called us, and my mother picked up the phone.

"Is this Jean-Claude's mother?" the priest asked.

"Yes. This is she."

"Your son is with me. I am Father Dupont. I live in Toulouse."

"Oh my God. Did you find him?"

"No, he stopped at my church. He's really in bad condition. You have to come to pick him up."

"Yes, Father. I am going to send his brother Ernest. Give me your address please," Mom said.

Toulouse was about six hours by train from where we were living. My mother immediately asked Ernest to go find him. Two days later, both of them came back home. Jean-Claude was in really bad condition emotionally and physically; he wasn't himself anymore. We wondered what had gone wrong with his mental health. We were devastated and didn't know what to do. I didn't know what to think about it. I thought my mother felt helpless and needed some help, but was it a good option to send him to Africa? I asked myself, "Why not let him stay in a hospital in France?" Technology was more sophisticated in France than in West Africa.

One day, when I was by myself, I received a call from my aunt in Africa. It was very unusual for her to call unless something very important happened. She didn't tell me anything; she asked for Jacques. Of course, we talked for a little while, and she asked me about the children.

"Hello, Annick. How are you? Is Jacques in?"

"No, he's not in. Why, Tantie?"

"I need to talk to him. Let me call back later, okay?"

"Okay, Tantie," I said.

When I finished my conversation with her, I wondered, *Why didn't she tell me exactly what was going on? Why did she only want to talk to Jacques?* Her call worried me.

When Jacques came home around one thirty p.m., I told him about my aunt's call.

"She didn't tell you why she called?" he asked.

"No, she didn't," I said, "and I don't like this!"

Around three p.m., the phone rang again. I was in the kitchen, and Jacques took the call in the bedroom. I heard him talking to my aunt. Their conversation last for about ten minutes. After the call, he came in to tell me about it.

"Annick," he said, "something happened to Jean-Claude."

Worried, I asked him, "What do you mean? What happened?"

"Jean-Claude passed away two days ago at the hospital."

"At the hospital? What are you saying?"

I couldn't believe what I was hearing—my brother Jean-Claude had passed away! Crying and yelling, I asked Jacques to call my aunt again; I needed to talk to her. He wasn't okay with that, but I insisted. After five minutes, we called my aunt, and she explained to me the circumstances of my brother's death. I was devastated. I couldn't believe what she was telling me. My mind raced with questions: Why had someone close to me died again? What had I done to deserve this? I kept asking those questions, but I couldn't find any answers. I felt guilty about Jean-Claude's death, like I had about my mother's, even knowing that I hadn't done anything to provoke them.

My thoughts about Jean-Claude went back to when my mother was still alive. I had thought that he had it all—the job, the money, his apartment, his girlfriend. What had happened? I knew he was drinking and that he was mentally sick. After my father's suicide, everything had changed for everybody. *What a disaster,* I thought. I remember that, when I moved out of my family's home to my own apartment, he sometimes wrote to us all. He wanted us to send him newspapers and magazines from Paris to be updated on what was going on in France. He missed France enormously. I hadn't sent him what he wanted, and neither had my brothers because we didn't know how to help each other. Jean-Claude also wanted to come back to Paris. He asked us to buy a ticket, but we didn't do anything, because we thought he would be a burden for us.

I also remember that, after I was married to Jacques, he asked me the same thing; he wanted to be in Paris with our family. At the time, I talked to Jacques about it, but he didn't approve at all. He said, "That isn't a good idea." "It isn't a good idea for whom?" I asked myself. I thought Jacques didn't want to feel responsible for my brother in case anything happened to him.

I felt so bad about it, because we didn't support him. If my brothers and I had been more supportive of each other, we could have done something for Jean-Claude. I carried this guilt for a long time, as though it was my responsibility to support or provide for everybody. I carried Jean-Claude's death with me for many years. I cried for days. I went through depression again.

We got another call from my aunt saying the funeral would be in two weeks. Jacques bought a ticket for me to go to my brother's funeral in Africa. He couldn't go because of his job. We asked Georges and Julia to take care of the boys, and they accepted. I felt relieved and grateful to have them in my life.

My flight to Africa was booked, and I waited for the day to fly. My depression wasn't getting better, though I wasn't drinking. It was very difficult to deal with my feelings, because they were mixed. I felt angry at my aunt because, in my point of view, she hadn't really taken good care of my brother. I was also angry at my brothers and myself because we hadn't helped him when he needed us. My sadness was overwhelming, and I kept asking myself, "What's going on with my family? I am losing everybody." I saw death as abandonment by my parents and my brother.

My flight was on a Thursday morning, and I took a taxi to the airport. There was no direct flight from Chicago to Africa, so I had to have a layover in Paris, where I meet my brothers at the airport for a few hours and from there, I flew to Benin. I arrived in Benin on Saturday morning, and the funeral was in the afternoon. My aunt was at the airport to welcome me. I had so many questions to ask her. I didn't want her to feel that I was accusing her of anything, though.

Slowly, I got ready for the funeral. I hated that time. I wanted everything to be over with.

I cried during the funeral. My cousins from my father's side weren't there, and I was shocked, but I didn't say anything; I didn't want to make any trouble. I wasn't feeling strong enough to confront people. Everybody looked at me because I cried so loudly. I asked myself why they weren't showing any emotion. "Didn't they love my brother?" I asked myself.

After the ceremony, someone explained to me that, in Africa, they didn't necessarily see people dying as a tragedy. They saw it as deliverance. I thought, *Now he's at peace.* It was difficult for me to accept that reality. I felt very empty. I wanted everybody to cry for Jean-Claude. When the funeral was finally over, I felt relieved. I will always feel sadness when I think about Jean-Claude because of a feeling that we should have done more for Jean-Claude, that we had given up on him. I lived with these sad feelings for many years.

We went back to my aunt's house when the funeral was over. I wanted to get away from everybody and from my sadness, my fears, my insecurity, and mostly, my brother's death. I still had a lot of fears about my past. I wondered why Jean-Claude had changed the way he had after our father's death. My brothers and I hadn't had any luck in being a happy and healthy family. The questions I kept asking myself were: how come they didn't take care of Jean-Claude more seriously, what really happened, and how did he really die? I thought his death could have been avoided, but I kept these fears and questions to myself.

My memories of Jean-Claude were still uncertain about the way we had gotten along.

The next morning, I had to fly to Chicago, but before that, I wanted to take a walk in the city and smell the ground, smile at the people, talk with them, and eat the great food. I still missed the feeling of warmth from my people. Mostly, I wanted to be by myself and think about everything that had happened. I wanted to think about my life and my family, knowing that I came from three different countries—Africa, France, and the United States. *Who am I?* I wondered. *Where do I come from?* I had so many questions about my identity. I became an independent thinker, and I couldn't stop thinking. My brain was always running. Above all, though, I had too many negative thoughts.

At that time, I didn't have the urge to drink. After Jean-Claude's death, it was like I was in retreat. I wanted to heal from my childhood and the losses of my parents, Christian, and Jean-Claude, from my drinking problem and the attempts at suicide, and from the loss of my first child. I hadn't healed after any of those problems, and I didn't know how to do it. Somehow, though, there was a power of survival inside of me. My desire to keep going was very strong. I didn't know it at the time. I sure didn't know who I was then. If some people in my life had have given me some love, taking care of my emotional needs and trying to understand me, I am sure I wouldn't have been so insecure.

When it was time for my flight, I said good-bye to everybody and promised them I would come back. I was relieved and glad to go back to my life and my children, whom I was missing a lot. I had to go back to Chicago. My connection from Benin and Paris was immediate; I didn't have to wait. I arrived in Chicago the next day. I was very tired but happy to be home. Deep in my heart, I knew that Chicago, my new town, was the place where I would find peace and happiness but always with some difficult experiences. It wouldn't be my final destination, I thought, but Chicago would be the place where I would start my spiritual journey. I didn't know how, but I would find it there.

Jacques and the boys were waiting for me at the Chicago airport as were Georges and Julia. I was so glad to see them. An unusual feeling took me—I felt lucky. I wanted to keep that feeling forever. I wanted to freeze that feeling for a long time, to be with it.

But I still felt an emptiness when thinking about Jacques. I didn't know if our marriage would survive, but I was willing to try to make it work, because for a long time if something wasn't right, I had felt it was my fault. My parents and siblings made me feel that way. I didn't know if Jacques wanted to save our marriage. Maybe he didn't feel any love for me.

One thing I really knew was that I had to get some help for my drinking problem.

My Recovery from Alcoholism

THINGS WERE FINE FOR A while, and I was enjoying my children a lot. We saw Georges and Julia a lot because our children played together.

We decided that Jacques and I would move out of the apartment and buy a house with a pool, because he was doing very well in his job. We asked for the help of a real estate agent. Her name was Patricia. She was very good at what she did. It took us about four weeks to find a very nice house. It was in Palatine, which was five minutes away from our apartment. I really loved the house. It was a ranch with four bedrooms and a furnished basement. After buying it, we meet the previous owner, who was single. Two weeks later, the house was ours. The boys had their own bedroom.

I thought that, by buying this new house, maybe Jacques and I would have new things to do together. That wasn't the case, though because we felt more and more tension when we lived together. The children felt it too. They were growing up really fast and becoming smarter and smarter. Unfortunately, we were arguing in front of them, which wasn't good at all. Being together became more difficult. *Why did he become that way? Was it because of our move to Chicago?* I wondered. I knew I wasn't meeting his expectations, because he wanted me to be a certain way. I didn't want to be that way, because it wasn't who I wanted to be. My tendency was to rebel, and I was very stubborn. I also found any excuse to drink; I drank for bad or good feelings at any moment, and Jacques knew I drank behind his back.

One day, he came to me with an ultimatum: "If you don't stop drinking, you are going to lose your family. You have to choose between us or the drink."

"Okay," I said, "I am going to get some help."

I was scared enough of losing everything that I wanted to get some help. Jacques never came to me to ask me why I was drinking or what my real problem was. I took it very seriously, and in two days, I pulled myself together to seek help. I was sober for two days by the time I picked up the phone. I called a hotline number for drug and alcohol use. Jacques stood next to me while I was on the phone.

I don't know why, but I was scared. I was scared of stopping drinking, and I wondered what my life would be without drinking. *Am I going to have fun if I am sober? Will I be able to stop drinking completely?* I didn't really admit to myself that I was an alcoholic. I wanted to get some help because Jacques had given me an ultimatum. I didn't call the number on my own steam, because I didn't recognize I was an alcoholic; that makes all the difference. A lot of questions ran through my mind.

I finally talked to someone on the phone, explaining, "I want to get some help, because I have a drinking problem."

"Okay, we do have some AA meetings you can go to. You will need a sponsor."

"What is a sponsor?" I asked.

"A sponsor is someone who will be there to support you emotionally in case you have an urge to drink," the person said. "If this is the case, you will have to contact her immediately. Madam, what is your address? I am going to send you someone. That way, you can talk with her. Let's choose a date and time, okay?"

"Yes, I would like that," I said.

A couple was supposed to meet me in two days. I was so nervous about it that I couldn't sleep. So many questions went through my mind. "Am I really ready to stop drinking?" was the most important question that I could have asked myself, because I didn't want to be in denial either. Another question came to my mind: "Had I somehow hurt my children and Jacques?" My answer was yes, maybe emotionally. Again guilt came to me. Was I an alcoholic like my father had been? When I thought about him, a feeling of anger came to me. The difference between him and me was that he hadn't gotten help like I was going to. *Yes*, I thought, *I need to get some help*. It was a difficult and stressful period of my life. I was so damaged from my past. I wondered how I was going to get well. Actually, my first step would be to stop drinking, and the rest would follow with the help of God.

Two days later, the couple came to my house. I let them in, and we talked for about one hour. I told them my story, and they asked me why I wanted to stop drinking. They told me their stories as well and how and why they had stopped drinking.

Jacques wasn't with us, and I hadn't asked him to be there. Alcoholism is a family disease, though, and when I think about it, it would have been nice if he had been included at the meeting. I had to educate myself about the real source of my mental disease. The couple told me the place and time of where to attend AA meetings. I felt overwhelmed by all the information; I had to accept the fact that I was one of them. Was I really ready to accept myself as an alcoholic? A different kind of fear took over.

The couple asked me to meet them in Palatine for a meeting. They said they were willing to pick me up to make sure I would be there.

Two days later, they came. I was ready to go to the meeting. The drive there from my place was about twenty minutes, and the meeting was at ten thirty. We arrived there at ten fifteen. When we got there, there were different groups of people at each table. I followed the couple to a table where people were already seated. There were about eight at the table. The meeting started at ten thirty sharp. Someone went to the podium and started to talk into the microphone.

The meeting started with words from the book of *Alcoholics Anonymous*

The speech was very new to me, and I had a hard time understanding it. The words were very deep and meaningful. I heard a lot the word *God*, and I liked it because, for years, I had felt very close to God. I was comfortable talking to him, and he was included in my little world.

I thought the first step for me would be to admit that I was powerless and that I needed God in my life. I needed to be honest with myself. I also needed to admit that I was an alcoholic who needed help.

After she was done talking, each group started its own meeting, and each person around each table had to say something. It was the first time

I had attended an AA meeting. The couple I had come with asked me to listen, so I didn't talk; I couldn't because of my fears about being heard.

The things I heard during the meeting were very interesting. Actually, it was more like a therapy group where you have to talk about your past drinking. At the end of the meeting, I felt very overwhelmed, and I didn't know what to think. I told myself, "I am not like these people. I am not an alcoholic!" I was wrong; I was one of them. The more I listened to the others, the more I identified myself with them. It was frightening.

When the meeting was finally over, I needed to find a sponsor, but I didn't know anyone yet. The couple I came with found one for me and introduced me to her. I had to contact her each time I had an urge to drink or wasn't feeling good. Then the couple I had come with drove me home.

"Annick," they said, "if you ever need something or you have a question, please call us. If you want, we can pick you up for another meeting."

"Yes," I said. "I would like that."

They would pick me up again in three days.

When I got inside, I talked to Jacques about the meeting. All he said was, "That's good."

We didn't talk a lot, and he didn't ask me any questions while I was taking care of the children whom I had missed a lot. After a while, I put them to bed. Then I went to my bedroom and meditated. I thought a lot about what I had heard at the AA meeting and the need to be true to myself. I wanted to change for myself and for my family—the alcoholism first. Once the alcoholism changes, everything around it changes. I realized that I couldn't manage my own life, and wondered how I could manage my own family.

The day of my second AA meeting came, and the couple was on time to pick me up. We went to the same place but not the same table. The meeting started on time, and this time, I wanted to talk. I introduced myself and talked about why I drank. Everybody listened. I felt very uncomfortable, because I wasn't used to being listened to. Suddenly, tears came to my eyes, and I couldn't finish what I wanted to say. I cried, cried, cried, and the lady next to me took over.

After the meeting, the couple dropped me off at my house. Jacques didn't ask me anything about the meeting; it was like he wasn't interested.

I didn't feel any support from him. He thought he didn't have anything to do to save our marriage, and he made me feel like it was all about me. He was wrong. I was emotionally drained, and all I wanted to do was go to bed.

I didn't tell anyone I was going to AA meetings, not even my dear friends Georges and Julia. I felt ashamed of it.

When Florian was nine years old and Vincent seven and half, we decided to sign them up for soccer. They were so cute in their soccer uniforms and excited to get started that it was hard to stop their enthusiasm. They weren't on the same team, because of the difference in their ages. When they had their first practice, I felt so proud of them. I sat by myself on the grass where I could see them playing. A Lady Teresa Hunt sat down next to me, and we smiled at each other. The smile she gave me warmed me deeply. She made me feel like I wanted to talk to her, and after a while of shyness, I decided to introduce myself. Even now, I knew I was meant to meet her, because she became my closest friend.

"Hello. I am Annick," I said.

"Hi. How are you? I am Teresa, Teresa Hunt. So your boys also play soccer? What team are they on?"

"I believe Florian, who is just right there, is on the same team as your son, and Vincent, my other son, is there."

"Oh, yes. I see them!"

That was the beginning of a long relationship. Teresa was tall and very attractive with green eyes. She was well-spoken and funny. She was a teacher of kindergarten children, and she studied psychology. Teresa was married and had three children. She lived in Palatine very close to me, about five houses away from my house.

For the time that I talked with her, I felt like I could trust her. It was like I had known her for a long time, because she made me feel comfortable. We talked and laughed the whole time the children played soccer.

When the practice ended, we introduced the children to each other. I was glad for my boys to have a new friend in Philipp, Teresa's son. Teresa Hunt was always there for me when I had some difficulties in my life, and she still is.

We promised each other to get together with the children on the weekend. She invited us to come to her house, and I looked forward to it. After meeting her, I went home with my boys and told Jacques about how I had met Teresa Hunt.

The next day, I felt an urge to go to an AA meeting, because I had an urge to drink again. I sat down at a table with more than ten people. After hearing a young man talk about his behavior when drinking, it was my turn to talk, but I couldn't again. Tears started to come as I was just sitting around the table being watched and listened to. I asked to talk later. When my turn to talk came again, I talked about my parent's death. I felt the need to talk about my past more than about my drinking problem. After the meeting was over, I was glad to go home.

I kept going to meetings every other day. Jacques didn't like it so much, because I wasn't with the boys taking care of them. I thought it wouldn't bother him, because it was for the sake of myself and the family, I couldn't understand his reaction. He seemed afraid that I would be influenced by others. The more I went to meetings the more I felt better, and he didn't like it.

I made some friends at AA, and most of the time when we got together, we gossiped. It felt a little awkward, because I didn't know them that well.

When the weekend came, my children and I met with Teresa. The weather was nice, so the children played outside. Teresa and I decided to cook something for lunch, and we talked and talked. We had very deep conversations, and she became my confidante because I related to her. I talked about anything with Teresa. She listened to me even about things that were missing in my marriage. I talked to her a lot about my marriage and the fact that I was unhappy with myself first. I envied her lifestyle and her confidence. To me, her marriage was the picture of a good marriage; she had good communication with her husband and her children. I wanted that in my marriage with Jacques, but I felt I was the only one working on my marriage.

All the couples I knew seemed to have good marriages and I wanted that so deeply that I was envious of them, envious of what they had. I asked myself, "Why do I have to be in marriage where I am crying all the time and feel so unhappy?" At that moment, I knew I didn't have a marriage. I was living with someone with whom I had almost nothing in common. I was with someone who wanted to control me. I wanted to be free, respected, and loved. I didn't feel I had that. It became a necessity for me to take care of myself and my boys.

Then I was a month sober and proud to be. I felt very good about it. Since the day I had stopped drinking, I had praying to God every night to help me stay sober one more day. The program said to take it one day at the time. I also asked God to help me in my marriage, to help Jacques to change, to open his heart. I was suffocating in our marriage. I couldn't go anywhere because, for a long time, he gave up on me. Each time I wanted to do something, I had to ask him. I didn't like it. I wasn't working, and if I needed some money, I had to ask him for that too. Sometimes, I needed to go to a meeting in the evening, and he didn't like that either, even if he didn't say anything at the beginning. I was worried for the boys because they were growing up in a bad environment. We argued all the time. I told Jacques that I wanted to start working, because the boys were going to school all day. He didn't encourage me at all.

My meetings were going well, and I made some progress. I was on step three. I made a decision to turn my will and my life to over the care of God as I understood him. Yes, I needed God, my higher power, in my life. My new sponsor Peggy helped me a lot by working on my steps with me. I needed to be around people who had the same disease as me, and I needed to change my bad habits to good ones. My thought was to change little by little.

I also changed my diet. I ate healthier with more vegetables and fruits. When I wanted to drink something, I drank either water or soda. I made something else for the boys for lunch or dinner. Some days, it was a struggle to not drink. I suggested that Jacques stop buying alcohol and take away the alcohol we had in the house.

"No," he said, "I will keep the bottles in the house. You just have to be strong enough to not drink."

He didn't get it. He didn't understand the program and didn't want to, so I kept trying to be sober, knowing that I had alcohol in my house.

On a weekday, the boys were playing outside with their bicycles. The door to the house was open, and a lady named Nancy knocked on the door and introduced herself. She lived two blocks down from my house.

"Hello," she said. "My name is Nancy. I live just around the corner. I saw my children outside playing with yours, and I wanted to introduce myself to you."

"Oh yes, of course," I said. "My name is Annick, and my children are Florian and Vincent."

"I have one girl and a boy," she said. "This is a nice neighborhood, isn't it?"

"Yes, it is," I said. "I am glad to meet you Nancy."

I invited Nancy into the house and offered her something to drink. I liked her immediately. She was very nice and easy to talk to. Nancy had short blond hair and very tall and skinny with blue eyes. She was very attractive. Nancy wasn't working; she took care of her children and was very involved in church activities. We talked about our children and their activities. Her children were younger than mine, and they often played together.

It was soon time for her to go home, but we promised each other to get together very soon. When she left, I thought I was lucky because I had made another new friend. I felt like I could trust her, and she became another confidante of mine. It was she who reassured me when I was feeling down. We sometimes went to a Chinese restaurant called Yus Mandarin.

I remember Nancy stopping by to say "Hi," and we talked for about an hour. Before going home, she had written a number on a fundraising ticket she had bought a while before, and she had kept the second half of the ticket. After , dialing the number, I kept the ticket on my living room table. One evening while I was eating dinner, the phone rang. It was Nancy, who told me that the ticket with the number she had given me was a winning ticket from the fundraising event. She wanted me to receive the money, which was about two thousand dollars. I was so surprised by her generosity that I truly didn't know how to thank her. That was something that I will never forget.

At the time, I wasn't sleeping very well at night. I was on medication for anxiety, and I was taking sleeping pills. I still felt anxious and scared of the unknown all the time. I had realized a long time before that I had some personal issues and that I couldn't talk about it with Jacques, because our relationship hadn't been a good one from the beginning. I especially didn't know how to express my feelings. It was easier for me to talk to my girlfriends.

The more I went to AA meetings, the better I felt. I related to a lot of people in the group. We were all different with different social lives and stories, but we all had the same disease. I also learned that, when someone in the family was an alcoholic, the whole family suffered. That made me think about my relationship with Jacques and my children. I told myself, "Maybe Jacques wanted me to be more confident about myself. Maybe I don't know everything. Maybe, maybe." I asked myself all those questions. On the other hand, Jacques's actions toward me told me the opposite. Maybe living with me wasn't easy because I was an alcoholic. What I am saying is that I was and still am a good person; people, including Jacques, had been taking advantage of me. I recognized that I wasn't always patient with my children, and they felt it. I believed that things were wrong because of me, and then I felt guilty.

One of the prayers I really loved was the Serenity Prayer. It says, "God grant me the serenity to accept the things I can't change, courage to change the things I can, and wisdom to know the difference." It was like I was asking God to give me clarity by accepting things, people, events, circumstances, and places I couldn't change, to be able to change the things I could—me, my attitude, my way of thinking, my ability—and to know the difference. It was very powerful for me. I thought everybody could use this prayer. My recovery from drinking was changing the way I was thinking, along with my diet and my relationships with Jacques and others including my children. I became more rebellious against Jacques. I didn't accept his put-downs most of the time anymore, and I tried to stand up for myself.

When I reached two years of sobriety, he made me stop going to AA meetings. The worst thing about it is that I listened to him. My confidence wasn't quite there yet. If I didn't listen, he made my life hell, and it was already hell. My friends from AA called and asked me why they weren't seeing me anymore. I felt really bad, as though I didn't have any power or strength.

The days passed, and one day when I was in the kitchen cutting pineapple, Jacques and I argued. I felt so overwhelmed that I had an urge to drink. Yes, I picked up my first drink again. He insulted my brother Jean-Claude, who had passed away a while before. I reacted very strongly because no one could insult my brother to me.

I was doing my best to take care of my kids. One thing I knew for sure was that Florian and Vincent didn't have all my attention as a mother, because I wasn't myself. I felt very guilty about that. Another thing was that I didn't want to raise my kids the same way as my mother had raised me.

More days passed, and on a Saturday, we were all invited to a party at the home of one of our neighbors, and of course, I knew alcohol would be served. As soon as we arrived, Florian and Vincent went to play with other children. Jacques and I spent the whole time away from each other. He was with one group of people, and I was with another. He left the party just after dinner and took the children with him. I stayed, because I wanted to drink and be away from him. I didn't even participate in conversations. I just listened and drank. After a while, I got so tired and sleepy that I went to sleep under a table in another room. I remember when I woke up, because someone drove me home. When I got home, I went directly to bed.

The next morning, I woke up with a headache and argued with Jacques. Of course, he made me feel bad, telling me how embarrassing my attitude was. I was so sad and angry that I cried for almost the whole day. He ignored me more and more, and he decided to not do anything with me anymore. Our sex life became nonexistent; we didn't have sex for quite some time.

I tried to hide my sadness from my children, but they were at an age when they knew something was wrong with their parents. My children were growing up very fast. I missed them from the bottom of my heart, but I wasn't there emotionally for them.

My life at home was more difficult with Jacques ignoring me. I wasn't working, because I was still trying to be a housewife and parent for my children. We had two cars, and he drove an old Toyota to work for a while and had bought a black Honda that was more secure to enable me to drive the children to school and activities. One day, for reasons he didn't tell me, he decided that I would drive the old Toyota and he would drive the black Honda.

"Why," I asked. "The Toyota makes too much noise. I don't trust that car, and I drive the children from place to place."

He didn't want to hear it. The garage couldn't hold both cars because of old stuff that was there. So the Toyota was parked outside all the time. In the winter, every time I needed to go somewhere, I had to remove snow from the car. I was so mad at him. I wondered why I was going through that, because it was not fair.

My children saw all of this; they saw me crying all the time. I wanted to hide my tears, but sometimes I couldn't. I needed so badly to be understood and to be loved. Thank God I could talk to my friends about what was going on at home. They listened. Julia and Georges also knew that things were not fine at home.

One day, Julia told me, "Annick, if you need to talk, I am here!"

"Okay, Julia," I said. "Thank you"!

Julia and Georges offered me a part-time job in their company. The job was very simple; I had to do classification. Their company was at home, and there were only six people working there. I worked three days a week while the kids were at school. I got a little money for myself, and I loved it because I got out of the house and got to see other faces. I knew that Julia and Georges didn't judge me. I felt more comfortable with them than with Jacques. Isn't that sad?

In my third week of working with them, when I got back home, Jacques said to me, "I need to talk to Julia and Georges. I am going to see them."

"Why do you need to talk to them? Is there something wrong?"

He didn't answer me. He took the car keys and drove to Julia's house. I was so worried that I immediately called Julia and Georges.

"Julia, I don't know what's going on, but Jacques is coming to see you."

"Do you know what he wants to talk about?"

"No, I don't know, but I am scared. I am sure it's about me!"

Actually, I was right, because when Jacques left Julia's house, she called me back quickly to let me know that he didn't want me to work anymore because I wasn't taking care of the house and the children enough. He complained that the house was a mess. Julia said couldn't believe what she heard from him. At that moment, their respect toward Jacques started to degrade. Julia thought I was an adult, so the decision needed to come from me.

When Jacques came back from Julia's house, he said, "Well, I am sure Julia told you why I went to see her. You have to stop working there!"

"Why," I asked. "The children are in school when I am working. What's the problem?"

Sometimes, I smoked outside, and he didn't like it. One day while it was still winter, I felt the urge to go smoking. Jacques saw me outside, and when I finished my cigarette, I tried to get inside but the doors in the front and the back were locked. I went back to the front door. My children could see me. I made some gesture to ask them to open the door, but they had been told by their father not to open the door. I felt really bad for them having to see me like that outside on a snowing night. I stayed there for about ten minutes. After that, Jacques opened the garage, but not the house door. To be warm, I stayed in the car for about ten minutes until he opened the door. I screamed at him and cried.

"Why are you treating me like this, like a dog? What did I do to deserve this?"

"You are not listening to me," he said.

"Go to hell!"

I didn't want to sleep in the same bed, so I went to sleep in the furnished basement. Before doing that, I made sure that the children were asleep. It's unnecessary to tell you that I was drinking more and more, and of course, I was still hiding it. Before relapsing, I had been sober for two years and proud of it. But I wasn't talking to my AA friends anymore, and they weren't calling me at home.

Sometimes, I took the children for walks to meet with our neighbors. That helped me hide my sadness, but I believe they knew that I wasn't happy. I became very skinny and looked older because I wasn't eating correctly; instead, I was drinking. Teresa was worried about me because I was losing weight. I told her and Julia and Georges everything. Jacques didn't seem concerned. I don't even know if he noticed anything.

One day, I needed to buy some personal stuff for myself, and I had to ask for money. He didn't have the courtesy to come and give it to me and instead asked Florian to give me the money.

"Don't you ever put the children in the middle of this," I told Jacques. "They are already enduring enough of this!"

He acted like he didn't hear me. I knew that someday something would change. It wasn't a healthy way to live, especially with children.

I was suffocating, and I had nowhere to go. I felt like a prisoner in a nice house with a pool.

My Second Attempt at Suicide

In January of 2002, we were all in the house watching TV. Jacques and the children were sitting on the same sofa, and I was sitting by myself on another one. I felt loneliness and desperation, and my mind started to go crazy. My sick mind was saying, "I am sure that, if I disappear, nobody will miss me."

I wasn't thinking about anything else, and I decided to do the unthinkable, the irreparable: I wanted to end my life. The sad thing is that I wasn't thinking about my boys; I was being selfish. I wasn't even thinking whether my action would be judged by God. I just wanted to escape from my pain, which nobody could understand except me. It was a pain that I wanted to escape for the rest of my life, because I was still an alcoholic. At that time, I was really desperate. While I write this, I know that what could have saved me from doing such a thing was going to an AA meeting. My action was more of a cry for help than a real attempt at ending my life. Before doing it, I called two people—my brother and sister-in-law. My sister-in-law immediately called from North Carolina for an ambulance.

I took enough sleeping pills to make me sleep and not think about anything. Before taking the pills, I said, "Please, God, forgive me for my action."

There is no excuse for what I did. I could have found another way to deal with my situation. I didn't tell anyone about my action other than my brother and sister-in-law. God knew how much I was suffering and my state of mind. I was an alcoholic. I just repeated what my father had written when he had committed suicide. This disease is in my family, and the suffering in my marriage didn't help either.

After I took the pills, I woke up at a hospital in Rolling Meadows. The amazing thing is that I woke up all refreshed. I was at peace. It was like I had seen a white light. I felt a peace in my heart that I will remember all my life. I lay in the bed and felt the light of day on my face. It was a very spiritual moment and feeling, though it's difficult to explain. One thing that I know for sure is that I went to the other side. I went home to a place where only love can be found. It was like someone telling me, "Annick, it's not your time to come home. You haven't reached your destiny." I knew that God had forgiven me for my action. While I write this, I feel tears coming as I remember it. I had God on my side.

A nurse on my right side was smiling at me. I smiled back. That smile made me feel comfortable. It was a smile that I will always remember.

The doctor who took care of me came to visit me, to find out how I was doing. He was tall, and he caressed my face as he said, "Hey, we need you here."

I cried when I heard those words. A stranger who didn't know me was telling me that; it was something to me. How many times had I wanted and needed my parents, brothers, and even Jacques to tell me those words?

The same day, Julia called me at the hospital. I felt so embarrassed that I found an excuse not to talk.

"Julia, I am sorry. Can I call you back?"

I was in my little world, and coming back to reality was very difficult. I just wanted to be alone.

Later on, Jacques came to visit me. He was the last person I wanted to see. I threw a book at him and yelled, "Get out. Get out. I don't want to see you!"

He disappeared after hearing those words.

The nurses and the doctor took care of me, and that was what I wanted: someone who could take care of me. But it couldn't go on for too long, because I had to go home.

The day came when Jacques came to pick me up, and I said good-bye to everybody. Before I could leave the hospital, I had to stop at the office. They wanted me to schedule psychiatric treatment for an aftercare program.

When I got in the car, Jacques said, "You know, after this, you are not going to find a damn job. Didn't you think about the children when you did this?"

I stayed silent. The only thing I thought was, *Yes, I didn't think about the children.* They saw everything with the ambulance coming to the house. I traumatized them and felt guilty for a long, long time. I thought, *"This is all he's telling me?"*

When we got home, the children were there waiting for me. I hugged them like I hadn't seen them for a long time. I got the feeling that they were looking at me with new eyes and I wanted to know what was in their minds. Thinking about this still hurts me.

That evening went too fast. When it was almost bedtime, I took care of them and put them in bed. Jacques didn't talk to me the whole evening, thought we slept back to back. The next morning, he went to work. It was very difficult to face the reality and consequences of my action.

Julia came to visit me, and it was a comfort to see her. She let me talk for hours about my feelings. We spent the afternoon together, and I didn't feel like she was judging me. She left before Jacques came home. The children came back from school at three thirty, and I made them a snack. I helped with their homework, and I prepared the dinner. I had a conversation with my children about what had happened to me and told them that I was sick. I don't know what Jacques had told them. I reassured them that it wouldn't happen again and not to worry about it.

My sister- and brother-in-law called me to ask how I was doing. I felt more comfortable talking about it with my sister-in-law. They really didn't know what to say to me.

The next morning, I went to the hospital for the aftercare treatment. I was there at nine a.m. I opened the door to the room, and many people were there already. I knew that all of them were there for the same reason I was. There were at least twelve girls. I sat down in a chair next to a girl who smiled at me. I smiled back at her. I didn't feel comfortable in the room, though.

A while later, a man came in the room and introduced himself.

"Hello, everybody. I am Doctor Wrung. I am a psychiatrist for the aftercare program. We are going to work together by talking, doing some activities—like painting, drawing, listening to some music—to help you release your feelings. I want you to feel comfortable with each other, because it's going to be a long program. First of all, I want you to introduce yourselves to each other. Sandy, why don't we start with you?"

Sandy introduced herself, starting, "Hello, I am Sandy … "

Then it was my turn to talk. I was very embarrassed. I didn't want to talk and tell them why I was there. But I wanted to be true to myself and not lie for any reason. The program was about our own feelings. We had to be honest with ourselves.

After everybody had been introduced, we had a break for ten minutes. After the break, Dr. Wrung asked us to go to another room. When we got to the room, another staff member was there as well. There were some paintbrushes, papers everywhere, some paintings, and a music player. The room was very peaceful.

"Hello, everybody," the staff member said, "I am Jack." *Jack again?* I thought. "You are here to do some painting and whatever you like. We have everything here. Make your choice, and pick everything you need to start painting. The first exercise will be to paint or draw what comes to your mind. Okay?"

All of us gathered what we needed to get the project done. I took some watercolor paints, a brush, and paper. It was the first time I was being introduce to painting and different kinds of media. I didn't know what to paint. I contemplated everyone for a while, and what came to my mind was a flower with different colors. I tried to paint a rose with different tones of purple. While I was painting and listening to the music, I found that I was in peace and harmony. The music was soft and slow. What amazed me was that I didn't have any difficulty painting the flower. It came out naturally, and I was surprised. I didn't want to paint something else; I just wanted to focused on the rose and make it perfect like I wanted to be.

An hour and a half later, Jack asked us to show our work to each other. What I saw were birds, places, houses, flowers, and landscapes. Everyone said "Wow" to each painting. I really loved the class.

It was already three p.m., though, and it was time to go home. Our next meeting would be in two days.

When I got home, it was time to pick up the children. I followed the usual routine—have snack time, help the boys with homework, play with them, and make dinner. Jacques didn't ask me anything about my class. I kept looking at the flower that I had painting and put it on the living room table, hoping that he would complement me on it. The thing was that I felt he was so detached from what I was doing or saying that I didn't feel like part of the family anymore except for taking care of the children and cooking for everybody.

One day, he told me, "In this house, you don't have a voice. You don't count."

When I heard those words, I felt like I needed to paint or draw. It was time for the children to go to bed, so after saying "Good night" to them, I went to the basement, took paper and a pencil, and started drawing something that came to mind. I wanted to experience again the good feelings that I had had when painting the rose at the aftercare program. This time, I didn't draw a flower but a seascape. The only problem was that I didn't have colored pencils.

While I drew, I experienced the same feelings of escaping from reality. I was in my own world of peace, love, tolerance, and justice. I found myself feeling things I didn't know I could. While I drew the seascape, my thoughts were that I wanted a new world of love and peace for everybody, but the most important was that I wanted to give love. While drawing, I thought, *How can I give love to someone else if I haven't experience it myself?* When I finished the drawing, I wasn't happy with the result, and I promised myself I would buy some colored pencils. It was nine thirty when I went to bed.

The next day, I stayed home thinking. I did a lot of thinking, especially about my suicide attempt. I know that, one day, I needed to face the question of why I had done it. Then I became very introspective. I was aware of my feelings, both good and bad. I wanted to find a solution by working on myself, that work would take the rest of my life. I had to convince myself that I was a good person and deserved love. This aftercare program would help me tremendously.

My brothers in France and my family in Africa knew what had happened to me. They didn't know what to say to me except that they felt sorry for me.

Days later, I went back to the aftercare program again. In the morning, we talked about our feelings. I remember that day clearly. I cried because I became aware of the inner work I needed to do to feel better about myself. I wanted to do it. Most of all, it meant going back to AA meetings. Staying sober would be very beneficial to me. I was moved by people's stories, and I was aware of their struggles; I wasn't the only one.

In the afternoon, we listened to some music. It was a peaceful music, and once again, I was in my own world. I couldn't wait until we would again paint. The day was almost at an end, and I was ready to go home to see my children.

While they had a snack, I went to the basement to draw again. This time, I took a book. It didn't matter which one, because I just wanted to see if I could copy an exact picture from the book. The book I had had a house on it, I copied it very well. This time, I was happy with the result.

I was very excited, because I wanted to see how far I could go in regard to drawing and painting. I wanted to bring every drawing I made to the aftercare program to show to everybody. They were impressed. I hadn't known that I had a talent for drawing, and my goal was to explore it more and more.

I also spent more time with Julia and Georges. We were having good time together.

When it was almost the end of the aftercare program, Dr. Wrung suggested that, if we needed more sessions, we have them in private in his office in Wheeling, and I thought that I needed that. That same day, we talked about our feelings again, and one last time, I cried. I was over thirty-two years old, and I had never talked about my feelings like at the aftercare program. It was all new to me, new and painful. After everyone had finished expressing himself, we painted again. Jack asked us to paint something very close to our hearts. Guess what? I painted another flower. I had discovered that I loved them.

When everybody was done with painting, Jack asked us to say what we wanted to become while looking at our paintings. I couldn't believe what I said: "I want to become a well-known artist."

Deep in my heart, I knew that something big would happen in my life. When the class was over, I promised myself I would buy some material for painting. My intention was to spend all my money to buy materials.

The next day, I went to an art supply store called The Starving Artist. I bought some watercolor paper and drawing paper as well as some pencils and watercolor paints. I also bought more colored pencils. I wanted to experience all kinds of media, but I knew I had to go slowly. I bought some art books to learn how to paint and draw. I spent almost all my money there, and I was happy about it because I knew I was going to experience good feelings and painting was an escape that I needed every day.

When I got out of the store, I went back home and into the basement. The basement became my refuge, and I spent a lot of time down there. I turned on some music, sat down, and started to draw from one of the books I had bought. I was so inspired and focused that every day I drew at least two pictures, always while the children were at school or when they played together or with their friends. I had discovered a new hobby that might become something more important in my life. I put all the pictures I made onto another table.

In pencil, I mostly drew portraits. I even drew my children and a mother holding her baby. I promised myself to frame that one. I just couldn't stop myself. Some of my drawings had a very spiritual feeling, and some showed anger, frustration, and sadness. The most common feeling was anger. Yes, I released some of the anger and pain from my childhood then. After each painting, I felt release and peace. I was becoming a "starving artist," and I loved it.

After two weeks of practicing with pencil, I then focused on watercolor. Again, I took a book, and I learned to paint from it. I found watercolors to be very delicate and difficult to use, but I liked the effect. With watercolors, I mostly painted seascapes and landscapes. I couldn't believe how easy it was for me to paint; it was like I had always done it. I believed that it had been in me for a long time. I believe that I was born with the talent. When I thought about it, my mind went back to when I was younger. I had a memory of when one of my teachers recommended that my mother encourage me to do something I was talented at. I know now that it was drawing.

My first private consultation with Dr. Wrung was on Monday and would be about twenty-five minutes from my house. He recommended that I see him twice a week and I was okay with that. The first time, we did some paperwork. The consultation was about fifty minutes long, so for the rest of the time, he asked me questions about my family and my past. I felt comfortable talking to him. He was very competent, and I knew I cry a lot during my sessions.

Jacques didn't know what to think about me painting so much. But it was something that he couldn't stop me doing, and he didn't talk to me about seeing Dr. Wrung either. I thought I was neglecting my children because of my obsession for painting, so I promised myself to spend more time with them. Yet I couldn't stop thinking about what I was going to paint next, no matter where I went or who I was with. I felt so good when doing it that I didn't know if somebody could understand.

For Christmas, Julia and Georges gave me an easel, and I was so happy about it. I could paint like a professional. Christmas wasn't my favorite holiday, but I put up a Christmas tree to make my children feel good about the holiday. I tried to show joy for them. Julia and Georges invited us over for Christmas day, and we had a good time. I also received Christmas cards from Nancy and Teresa.

During my second time with Dr. Wrung, he let me talk. I talked about things in general, but because we were in a therapy session, he asked me questions that required me to be honest if I wanted to get better. Because of my answers, I realized that I wasn't really ready to talk openly, and he let me know it. I promised to make an effort. I was afraid to remember everything that had happened in my childhood. I still didn't remember some things about my father and what he had done to me. My brain wasn't ready yet to face the truth about him. I remembered the beatings he had given to my brothers and me, though.

In the morning a week later, I touched my breasts while I was taking a shower. I touched the left one especially, and I felt something that hurt. I felt several lumps. Suddenly, I got scared, because my mom had died from a brain tumor that had started from breast cancer. I tried to convince myself that it didn't mean I would have the same thing. That whole day, I kept touching my left breast.

I talked about it with Jacques, saying, "I am going to see the doctor, because my left breast hurts."

All he said was "Okay."

I had been hoping for more support. I asked myself why I was hoping he would change his attitude toward me. I called a doctor and made an appointment for the next day. The rest of that day, I couldn't find the desire even to paint; I was very frightened. I talked about it with Julia, and she did her best to reassure me.

The appointment came slowly. I went to see the doctor at ten a.m. He consulted with me and asked me if the lumps hurt.

"Yes," I said. "They hurt me a lot."

He explained to me that, if the lumps hurt, it's not serious. He said that if they don't hurt, then there is a higher probability of a tumor. Well, they did hurt me, so I felt a kind of relief. The doctor he gave me a prescription to have the lumps removed, and for that, I had to go to the same hospital I had been to before. This time, I would go to the emergency room. He assured me that the operation would be very minor and quick, and I believed him. I had to go to the hospital two days later.

When Jacques came back home, I asked if he would drive me there, because the doctor told me to have someone drive me home after the surgery.

"I have to work that day," Jacques said.

I felt very hurt, but I asked Julia to drive me at the hospital. She was on time.

The surgery was very quick and didn't hurt at all, because I was asleep, but when I woke up, I felt discomfort in my breast. They told me to be very careful for several days until my breast healed. Then Julia took me back home. The surgery left a scar on my breast as the souvenir. I was glad to not have a cancer, though. During all of this, I thought a lot about my mother and about what she had been through. I wasn't there to support her, and I still feel guilt.

After the operation, I needed to rest while the children were at school. I had to pretend that nothing had happened.

One thing that I needed especially was to paint again. After using watercolors, I decided that it wasn't my favorite medium. I went back to the store to buy pastels. I loved the effect that pastels give. I practiced a lot with chalk and my main subject was flowers. I made a lot of progress. When I was working, I felt like I didn't have to make any effort to have the result I wanted, it was like my right hand was guided. It was so easy, and more and more pictures piled on the table. What I liked about pastels was that I could get my hands dirty. I loved that and the smell, which made me more aware of the media.

Learning something about yourself is one thing. Then I realized that I needed to be with others artists and have a teacher who can teach me other techniques. I wanted and needed to progress. I contacted an art teacher, and when I started my first class, I showed her some of my art.

"I can see that you are talented and your paintings are very spiritual," she said.

"Oh, thank you," I said.

I went to the art class once a week, mostly on Saturdays, for an hour and a half. The teacher had her own school, and I admired her for that. I was also very impressed by the way she taught.

I had another consultation with Dr. Wrung. This time, I talked about my parents and my relationships with them. I started to understand better why we had been a dysfunctional family. Dr. Wrung guided me by asking me questions that would make me go through the roots of the problems. It was very painful. There was all this pain and guilt that I had held onto during my life—the loss of my parents and my brothers Christian and Jean-Claude, my abortions, my father's sexual and physical abuse, and the negligence of my mother. I carried all this guilt, because I thought everything was because of me because I wasn't good enough. It was a lot; there was so much inner work for me to do for the rest of my life. At that time, I really felt that I was a victim.

I don't know where I found this inner strength, but I had it. God was with me. I knew it, and I asked myself, "Why is God making me go through all of this? What are the reasons for all of this?" Of course, I wasn't thinking about other people who suffered more than me. In that kind of situation, we think only about ourselves.

When I was at my most depressed, I pictured myself with God. He held me and told me, "Everything will be fine, Annick. You are not alone; I am with you. I will guide you to the happiness you deserve. Talk and pray to me. I will give you the strength and the courage you need to get through difficult situations."

Even now, I get tears in my eyes just thinking about it. I said the Serenity Prayer a lot: "God give me the strength to accept the things I can't change, to change the things I can, and the wisdom to know the difference." I talked to God all the time, saying, "God, please, give me the strength to change my marital life. You know that I am not happy, but I am worried for my children."

My Divorce

THE MORE I HAD MY private consultations with Dr. Wrung, talked to God, and did my artwork, the stronger I became. I knew that something had to change in my marital life, because I couldn't stay in my marriage. One day, I gathered the courage to talk to Jacques.

"You know, this is not a marriage that we have," I said. "Something needs to change."

"Yeah," he said. "You need to go to a psychiatric institute."

"But I am not crazy!"

"Or you go back to your brothers."

"How about the children?" I asked.

"The children will stay with me."

"How and when would I see them? You don't make any sense."

I couldn't believe it. He wanted me to go back to Paris to my brothers? It was like he had enough of me. His words made me feel like I didn't matter to my children. I was so furious and hurt by what he said. I promised myself that it would not happen that way. On that day, I made the decision to divorce him without telling him first. I didn't tell anyone about my decision, not even my close friends. The only person I talked to was God. I asked him to give me the strength and the courage to do it.

To do this, I first needed to go back to AA to get sober again. There was nothing Jacques could have told me to stop me from going to AA. At that time, I was still doing my best to take care of my children.

My first day back at AA was very helpful. I saw my old friends and new faces. I had to start from the beginning again, admitting that I was powerless over alcohol and that my life was unmanageable. It was a Wednesday, and the lady sitting next to me had been sober for twenty years. After the meeting, I asked her to sponsor me, and she said yes. We started working together. Her character was very authoritarian, and she reminded me of my father a little bit. I didn't pay too much attention, because she was there to help me, and I had to learn from her. Her name was Lisa.

My house was a place where I wanted to spend the least amount of time possible. I felt suffocating, unloved, frustrated, angry, and sad. I talked about it in AA and to my counselor as well. It was a subject that I needed to talk about, because it was part of my daily life. I cried a lot at AA. People felt uncomfortable about it, and someone mentioned it in a meeting.

"If I am crying," I replied, "it's because I have a lot in my heart, and I am cleansing myself from emotional baggage. AA teaches us to be tolerant with each other and not to judge."

I also made him aware that, when he started AA, he was probably in bad shape. I didn't know where those words came from, but I felt good after saying them.

Later, I made my brothers and family aware of my intention to divorce Jacques. They didn't like the way I was treated. In my marriage, I wasn't a saint either, because of my alcoholic background. I had some personal issues, but mostly, I was a person who needed to be there for myself.

I felt the urge to pray a lot, and I wanted some guidance from God. For about four months I felt the urge to go to church and pray after the children were at school. Even if I wasn't praying, I felt the need to be there. I needed the atmosphere, the spirituality, the smell of church.

I still painted, but I painted with anger and frustration. I even did a painting with the word *help* in pastel with different tones of blue.

When I decided to divorce Jacques, I thought about the consequences of my action. I thought a lot about my children. To me, staying in a relationship like that was not healthy to anyone. That there were some children was not an excuse. I didn't want to stay in the marriage because we had children together. I wasn't happy, and the rest of my family wasn't happy either. I had to found a solution to make my life better. Of course, I was scared. I was scared of losing my children, but it was a risk I had to take. I didn't know where the divorce would take me. The only thing I wanted was to get away from Jacques to find my sanity and my real self, and I didn't want my children to live in an unhealthy environment. I didn't want them to copy the same life as their parents.

On another day, I went back to church, and I sat there for over an hour.

"Tell me what I should do?" I asked God.

I knew he would support me in any decision I made, because we all have free will; we have the choice to make any decision. If we are convinced that what we are doing is right, then God will give us the courage and the strength to go thought with it. I knew I had to divorce, because I didn't want to cry or fear Jacques for the rest of my life. I didn't deserve to be unhappy. No one does.

One Tuesday, as I finished a painting, I cried and cried and cried. I felt so alone. I pulled myself together and decided to call someone to ask for some information about filing for divorce. I found a number in the yellow pages. I called it, and the person who answered referred me to an attorney who dealt with divorces. I called the number and made an appointment for a week later. I didn't know if I had called a good attorney. I didn't want people to know what was going on in my marital life, though, and I didn't want anybody to influence me. I felt vulnerable enough.

I started the divorce process in January 2001.

The day came when I would meet the attorney in downtown Chicago. The weather was cold but sunny. I took the train and walked to her office. I loved going to downtown Chicago; it felt like Paris with the big buildings and the people walking the streets. I arrived at the attorney's office and asked the secretary about her. She made me sit for a little while, and then the attorney came and greeted me.

"Hello, Annick. I am Laury. How are you?"

"I am fine. Thank you for asking," I said.

"Please follow me," she said.

Her office was small and well organized, though there were papers all over. She made me sit, and she asked me some questions about my life and marriage. She also asked me why I wanted a divorce. She took notes while she asked me questions. I found her very professional and easy to talk to. When she finished with her questions, she asked me to come back in two days. I was very scared, but I had to continue. When I left her, she gave me a big smile that said, "Don't worry. I will help you." I needed all the help I could possibly get.

I was in a hurry to get back to my children. I took the train to get home and was on time to be there for them. I tried my best to stay calm and to take care of them. Jacques and I didn't talk at all. When the children were asleep, I went to the basement to paint. I needed that. After painting, I prayed and asked God to give me strength and the confidence to pursue what I had started.

Days later, I went back to see the attorney, and we finished some paperwork. She asked me more questions.

"We have to file for motion for your divorce," she said then, "and your husband is going to receive a letter from me in two days."

"In two days? That fast?"

"Yes."

"What will happen after?"

"He has to appear in court in three weeks, and then the process will start."

"Oh my God," I said.

"If you have any questions, just give me a call, Annick."

I went back home crying. Suddenly, I wasn't sure about what I was doing, and I asked God to help me. I was home before the children got back from school. I let them play outside with their friends for a while, and then I started cooking dinner. I was very anxious and nervous.

Two days later, like my attorney had said, the postman rang the door at six p.m. Jacques opened the door, and when he closed it, he was holding the papers from my attorney. I was shaking like a leaf. I could see that he was very mad, because his face muscles were moving. He read the papers and looked at me. Then he went to his office. I could hear him talking on the phone. He came back into the living room and yelled at me.

"How dare you do that to me! It's going to be the war between us. You are going to lose everything."

I didn't say anything about his threats. After that moment, it was clear: we weren't speaking anymore, and the basement became my place to sleep, paint, and rest. I tried to stay calm in front of the children. I knew they were already disturbed by all of it.

I kept going to AA meetings, and I talked a lot about my divorce. I knew my disease would be a problem. I thought that, if I showed the judge that I was sober, it would be fine for me. My girlfriends from AA supported me a lot.

It was very difficult to stay in the same house with Jacques, knowing that we were going to divorce very soon. I decided to tell my other friends about it. They mostly told me that they were with me and that, if I needed them, they would be there for me.

The court date came. I had been talking to my attorney a lot before going to court, and I knew Jacques had done the same. The court wasn't too far from my attorney's office. Much to my surprise, Jacques's brother was there to support him. He had come from another state. I was shocked to see him, because I got along with him very well. I thought, *He hasn't even heard my version of the story, and he is standing by his brother.* I had to face the reality that he was Jacques's brother. I was by myself. I hadn't found it necessary to bring someone with me. I quickly sent a prayer to God and my mother and asked them to give me the strength to stand up for myself.

During the hearing, only the attorneys from each side spoke; neither Jacques nor I was allowed to speak. After the two attorneys finished speaking, the judge decided that Jacques would leave the house, and I would have custody of the children. Of course, Jacques protested the decision. He claimed that I was an alcoholic and an unfit mother. The judge decided to hire an attorney for the children and have me undergo a psychiatric evaluation. Jacques would have to finance all of this, because it had been his request, and he had to file another motion to get custody of the children. Things got very difficult for everybody, because I hadn't expected things to turn out that way.

After the hearing, I had to meet with my attorney again to talk about Jacques's motion. I expressed to her that he was lying about me. She explained that I would have the chance to defend myself.

After the hearing, I got home before Jacques. I needed to take care of the children and also talk to them about the divorce and what would happen. I was going to stay in the house for one year while going through all the procedures for the divorce.

Jacques came home very angry and said, "You are going to regret all of this, I swear!"

"We'll see about that," I said.

It took him about a week to find an apartment at International Village, which was not too far from the house. I complained in my mind about how big the house was, because it was a lot of work. The day he had to move out came, and he took all his clothes, his computer, and so on. None of his belongings were in the house anymore. He even took some furniture. He could have taken anything he wanted; I didn't care about any of that. What mattered to me was that I wasn't living with him anymore. I didn't know what the future would hold for me, but it was a start.

The papers from the judge stated that Jacques would be with the children every other weekend and holidays for one year until everything could be reevaluated.

The children's attorney called me and expressed the need to meet them. So I took them to her office in downtown Chicago. Her name was Judith, and her focus was on the well-being of the children, because they come first. Her decision would have a strong impact on which parent would be with the children.

A psychiatrist also called me to set up the appointment ordered by the judge. I had to do two evaluations, one by myself and another with my family. When I was in front of the psychiatrist, he asked me questions about my childhood. It was very painful to remember all of it, but I had to tell the truth about the attempts at suicide, my drinking problem, and so on. I felt like I was being judged because of my past, and I didn't feel good about it. My past was the result of who I was, but it didn't mean that I hadn't changed or that I was the same person. It didn't look good for me. The psychiatrist didn't evaluate Jacques, and Jacques's intention was to leave me without anything, because he was very determined to make me regret my decision.

My children's attorney met them twice—one time with me and another time with Jacques—and after those meetings, she would make her decision. I was so scared that her decision would be that the children would stay with their father. So far, my case wasn't very strong at all, and

I thought I would have little chance of being with my children after the year was over.

When I lived with my children, things were easier for me, because I found myself little by little. I spent a lot of money buying animals for them; they wanted hamsters, birds, and little lizards. Their desires for animals had come after their father had moved out, and of course, the house became a zoo. I was happy to do it, though cleaning the house wasn't my cup of tea. I was happy to see them happy.

It became routine for Jacques to take the children every other weekend. When they came back home, their attitudes would change, and I couldn't recognize them anymore. They didn't listen to me either; it was like they were being brainwashed. I tried to put myself in their shoes and admit to myself that they had been disturbed for a long time already and that the situation right then was not going to help them get better. At that moment, I felt an urge to put myself on my knees and pray for them, because they hadn't chosen this situation, they hadn't chosen to be born and to endure this. I tried my best to be there for them, and I had the strange feeling telling me that the boys preferred their father to me. It made me sad to think about it.

My AA meetings were going well. I had been six months sober when I started the divorce process. I didn't know if that was enough for the judge to let me stay with my children. When I think about it, my girlfriends from AA knew that I wouldn't be with my children because of my disease. Nobody told me. But one day when the children were asleep, I was on the phone with my sponsor talking about my divorce and how difficult it was. Suddenly, I realized.

"Oh my God, Lisa. I am going to lose my children. They are going to stay with their father!"

"Annick, do you want to come to my place and sleep here? I don't recommend you stay by yourself, and I don't want you to pick up your first drink either."

"No, that's okay," I said. "I won't drink."

"Are you sure?" she asked.

"Yes, I am."

"Okay. If you change your mind, call me, Annick."

After my conversation with Lisa, I cried and cried and cried like a baby. It was like a revelation to me. I was sure it had come from God. At that moment, I knew that the children would stay with their father. I also realized that it was in their best interest. Their father had a good job, and he was more emotionally stable. It was very difficult to admit that to myself.

Days later, I received confirmation from the psychiatrist's evaluation and the children's attorney. Both mentioned that it was in the best interest of the children to stay with their father. I was devastated. At that time, there were a lot of conversations between the attorneys and us. On that day, I decided to get used to the idea and to prepare myself to move out of the house after the year was over.

A court date was set up to read the verdict. It was that Jacques would be with the children. I wasn't happy with this, and I decided to contest the verdict. I asked the judge to do another evaluation. Only my mothering instinct pushed me to go further. This time, I had to pay for the evaluation, which would cost me more than three thousand dollars. Georges and Julia were on my side, and they were willing to help me financially. Remember when I said that you meet people for a reason? That was the case for Julia and Georges and all my closest friends.

The final evaluation was set up for a month later, and I was ready for it. While waiting for the evaluation, I tried to stay calm and take care of the children. It was very difficult. All the strength that I needed I got from my God and my friends and from myself. I didn't want to get too excited about this psychiatric evaluation. I wanted to think of the worst result as I would be prepared if it wasn't in my favor. This evaluation was important for me, because I wanted to believe that I had done all I could to stay with my children. I didn't want to have any regrets. My brothers supported me; they called me more than I expected.

While waiting for the evaluation, I kept painting. It was good for my soul. I tried a different medium, and I found oil painting very exciting to work with, because you don't need to frame the painting. On the other hand, it takes much longer for an oil painting to dry. My favorite medium was still the pastel.

During the procedures of the divorce, Jacques and I didn't talk. How could we? We felt too much anger and frustration toward each other. No one from his side wanted to talk to me; I became their enemy. It was the same on my side. Most of my neighbors knew that I was divorcing. To my great surprise, they said they knew I was unhappy, because I always looked sad, they never saw us together, and I was losing weight. I found that amazing, because they hadn't told me anything about their worries. I think they hadn't wanted to be involved in people's business, and I respected that.

The day for the evaluation came, and I went to downtown Chicago to do it with a different psychiatrist. It took about an hour and a half. I was getting tired of them asking me questions about my past, like I wasn't normal or like I had committed a crime. Actually, I couldn't complain because I had asked for this one.

After two weeks of waiting, the conclusion was the same as the first evaluation. They said that it was in the best interest of the children that they stay with their father. My attorney called me to let me know. Deep inside, I had been expecting it, and I had to face reality.

My attorney knew that I was painting, because I had been showing her some of my work. She was very surprised. She even showed them to the court. She comforted me a lot.

"Annick," she said, "I know it's very hard for you, but maybe it's meant to be. Maybe you need this time for yourself to get better. Try to make the most of it. It was a real pleasure to work with you, and I admire your bravery and your courage. You stood up for yourself alone."

I really wanted to die. I knew I had done my best, but it hadn't worked.

God was with me all the time, but the outcome still wasn't in my favor. He was telling me, "Annick, you need to be on your own and get back on your feet. The AA program will help you." I felt like he was also telling me, "When you feel better, your children will be with you. You haven't lost them. It's just the beginning of a new life with new adventures and new happiness." I wondered how I could be happy again without living with my children. They were my life, my strength, and my hope. *How can a mother feel when separated from her children? It's like dying*, I thought. I would never wish this on a mother, never.

The last court date was set up for a week later for the final decision. This time, I didn't contest anything. I knew I had done my best. Jacques's attorney offered me a settlement that the judge agreed to. The settlement meant that I had to move out of the house, that I would see my children every other weekend and for some vacations and holidays, and that I would be helped financially for three months, but after that I would be on my own. I didn't know how I was going to make it, because I only had a high school diploma with no experience of working in the States. I had to think ahead to make my life easier.

Jacques saw this settlement like he had won something, but I saw it as a way for me to get back on track and to have a new life. Of course, I felt devastated because of my children, but I was away from someone who didn't want to help me get better. I was free of him, and I was proud of myself because I had stood up for myself. All of this made me recognize that I had an inner strength. I had what it took to fight. I discovered a survival instinct in me.

I wanted to have a conversation with my children and explain to them that, no matter what, I would always love them and they would always be in my heart. Writing about this is still very painful. I didn't know if I would ever heal from my separation from my children. I told them that just because I was not living with them didn't mean that I wouldn't see them again. It was devastating, and we all cried.

The day I had to move out came quickly. I found a two-bedroom apartment twenty-five minutes away from my children's house. The rent was affordable. I didn't want my children to see me leaving like a thief when I moved out, so I made sure they were playing with friends and that someone was watching over them. My brother Charles came from Paris to help me, so I had to pick him up at the airport, and Georges drove me there. I was so happy to see my brother. For him, it was the first time in America. I wanted him to have a good stay as much possible, even with the circumstances of my divorce.

My apartment was very nice and clean, and I was on the second floor. The neighborhood was beautiful and quiet. Georges also came to help me to move in. I made sure to take all my clothes and some furniture. I was in bad shape emotionally, but I had to do it because I didn't have any choices. My brother's presence was very beneficial for me.

After moving out of the house, I put the keys in a safe place and told Jacques where they were and to pick the children up from their friend's house. Before that, I made sure to hug and kiss my children, before I had to go to my new apartment.

"Florian, Vincent, I love you," I said when kissing them. "I will call you very soon, and I will see you next weekend. Your dad will pick you up soon."

My heart hurt. I thought I was dying. It was so hard to pronounce those words; I didn't know if I would survive without seeing the children every day.

In the battle for my divorce, I had lost everything because of my drinking problem. I had lost my house and respect from others, and I wasn't able to see my children on a daily basis, but I got back my freedom. The program says, "When we get sober, the chance of losing everything is very high unless we have people supporting us like a spouse and friends." I was also aware that coming to a country where I didn't know the culture, systems, or traditions very well had been more difficult for me. I had been aware when filing that I didn't have appropriate support and help to file for divorce; I was on my own. Even if I had been supported well, would it have changed the outcome of my divorce? What was done was done. I was free. The only thing I would never heal from was separation from my children, and I was worried that they would forget me. I had to learn to live with the situation, and for that, I needed God's help. One chapter was over, and another was beginning.

I moved into my new apartment in 2003. It was so helpful and good to have my brother with me. We did a lot of work and were able to move all the furniture. I really liked the place. It was very cozy—a good size for me and my children.

Charles was able to stay with me for only one week. After that, he had to go back to Paris. I tried to take the most of it while he was with me. He really supported me emotionally, and I will be always grateful for it. We were also able to spend some time with Julia and Georges. When Charles had to leave on Sunday, Georges and I drove him back to the airport.

Then I was by myself, and I was deep in depression. I wasn't working, so my activities were going to AA, painting, and being in my apartment. Most of the time, I didn't want to get up in the morning, not even to take a shower. I was thankful that I did not feel the need to drink. It would take time for me to recover from the divorce. Being without my children was very painful, and I didn't know if I was going to survive. I especially needed to be careful of my financial situation. Despite all of this, I needed God's help more than ever.

I was in contact with Julia, Georges, Nancy, and Teresa a lot, and I was so grateful for them.

The first two years of living by myself were okay financially. I was very careful not to waste my money. I thought that I needed to find a job and that whatever came would be fine. My mind and actions were not in agreement. I thought that I needed to move on, to pull myself together, but my heart and body told me something else. I was grieving.

The first weekend after moving in came, and it was my time to be with my children. I needed to have some quality time with them. On Friday, I went to pick them up after school. They loved my place, but they complained because it was too far from their friends. Actually, they got used to it. During that weekend, I felt energized. I was having fun and felt hope. When I was with the children, I avoided saying bad things about their father. It was hard. I wanted to give them time to make their own judgments, and I knew it would take time. They slept in the same bedroom, and they were just fine. On Sunday morning, I felt kind of anxious, because I had to drop them off with their father soon; my stomach hurt.

As they got out of the car, I said, "Bye, Florian. Bye, Vincent. I will see you in two weeks."

"Bye, Mom," they said. "See you later."

"I love you, my babies. Never forget that, okay?"

As I drove back to my apartment, tears streamed down to my cheeks. Suddenly, I thought about my mom and how nice it would have been if she were still in the world.

The weeks went fast.

One night, I was lying in bed half asleep, when suddenly I had some memories about my father. I saw a tall man holding a little girl's hands and closing the door. I knew that the tall man was my father and the little girl was me. I had the feeling I knew things from people. I had had those feelings inside for a long time but never taken the time to really think about it. Now, they became stronger and stronger.

After I had those memories, I wanted to talk to Charles; he was the one I felt most comfortable with, maybe because we saw some things the same way. His thinking was outside the box like mine was. I made him aware of my memories, and he listened to me. He didn't try to tell me that I was making it up. No, he listened to me. While I talked with him, I felt anger toward my father. *How could he do that to me?* I wondered. After talking with Charles, I didn't know what to think about it all. I knew that one day I would talk to my therapist about it.

I spent a lot of time painting, now that I had some free time. I decided to do art shows in two different cities—one in Barrington and the other in Bartlett. I thought I had enough paintings to show. I needed time to frame them, title them one by one, and set prices. I talked to Teresa about it, and she was excited for me. She offered me a tent to exhibit my paintings in. The registration wasn't too expensive, and I really wanted to do it. More than one hundred people exhibited their paintings. I wanted my children to be a part of the show, but they couldn't come for some reason.

When we arrived at the art show, Teresa and I were very impressed by the other artist's work. I thought, *I don't have a chance competing with them*. I told Teresa about my feelings, and she said, "I am sure you will find some buyers."

My paintings were not common. Some reflected sadness and anger, and some reflected peace and light. It was like I was compelled to exhibit my work to the public.

The day went very well, and I was happy. I hadn't felt that way for a long time, and I didn't want the day to end. People stopped by to see my work.

"Hello," I said to them. "How are you?"

"I love your work," one said. "How much is this one?"

"This one is fifty dollars."

She bought it. I couldn't believe it. I felt very good about it. I needed those good feelings. Time went by, and I was having fun. Two other people bought some paintings. At the end of the day, I had $150. I thought, *I am going to keep this money to buy more material*. I was getting so tired that I wanted to be home already. Teresa and I packed everything. It was a hard work to do an art show.

When I got home, I was very hungry. I fixed myself something to eat, and then I went to bed. I didn't have the courage to unpack my material. It was already nine p.m. when I got into my bed. As I fell asleep, I thanked God for that day.

My Visions

I woke up suddenly at around nine thirty p.m., asking myself, "What's happening to me?" I had a vision of an old African couple, a man and a woman, for about three seconds. Their clothes were from my native country with a print that I will always recognize. They looked at me as though to say, "We are here." It was like they were watching over me. I felt peace when I had that vision; I wasn't afraid or scared at all.

After I couldn't fall asleep, I closed my eyes again. Five minutes later, something told me to open my eyes again, and then I had a magnificent vision of an old African man standing on my left side. This one lasted another three seconds. The old man had a long, white beard with long, white hair. He wore a gold dress that came to his feet, and he had a wooden cane in his right hand. Surprised but not scared, I sat up in my bed and tried to touch him, but he disappeared. The feeling I got from this vision was peace.

I had a hard time believing what I had seen. I thought I needed to talk about it with someone, but I thought that nobody would believe me. They would think that I was crazy, but I wasn't crazy. Something was happening. Questions ran through my head: "Who am I?", "Why do I have these visions?", and "What is the reason for all of this?"

At that moment, I promised myself I would keep a journal. It was one more secret I had to keep to myself.

Working at George's May

On June 2006, I received a call from a business consulting firm who wanted to hire me for a bilingual position. The job was a telemarketing position, and the lady asked me if I was interested in it.

"Hello, my name is Sophia," she said. "I am calling to ask you if you would be interested for a French, bilingual position."

"I don't know," I said. "Tell me more about it."

"We have some Canadian representatives who need some appointments in their area. This position has a base salary plus commission. What do you think?"

"Sophia, I don't know, because I have never worked in the United States."

"Why don't we set up an interview, and then you can decide if this for you or not?"

"Okay," I said. "What day and time?"

I didn't know if I wanted to go for this interview, but I wanted to try. The interview went well, and finally, I accepted the job. It was in a call center, and the company had about 150 employees. My job was to call the business owners of small-to-medium-size businesses to sell consulting services. I was very comfortable with that, because I had to speak French.

When my first day of work came, I was excited and nervous at the same time. I had to drive for about thirty minutes to get to work.

The manager introduced me to my new coworker, Sabrina. She was the only one who called Quebec in English to set up appointments for the team of five representatives in Canada. I sat in front of her, and she helped me. I was good at it. In one day, I was able to set up a total of ten appointments. I was proud.

Days later, I was asked to move to the second floor with other coworkers who were good employees, and I became one of them. I sat next to a photographer who was also from Africa. There were ten of us, and we got along very well. During lunch, we would get together and have homemade lunches or snacks. Those moments were precious to me, because they made me remember the good times I had had when working in Paris.

One of the representatives I got along very well with was Robert Lajoie. He was from Quebec and lived in Sherbrook. He has been there for me, listening to me, because at that time, I was still grieving for my divorce. With time, we shared ideas and comments about life, and one day, I talked about my own life—my feelings and fears and how I saw things. One of the reasons I was like that with Robert was because something told me he wasn't judging me.

He also asked me questions about my native country and my family. Little by little, he became my confidant. Since then Robert Lajoie has been in my heart. I will never forget him. Every year, he sends me a birthday card.

With time, I became familiar with the company, but I had some up and down moments. The company was very supportive, because they let me leave work earlier to be able to pick my children up from school.

In December of 2008, I was invited to visit another representative in Quebec. His name is Jean-Yves Ross. After we had been working together for a short period of time, talking on the phone sometimes, he gently invited me to spend the Christmas with his family. Of course, I accepted. For me, it was an occasion to visit Quebec.

On December 24, 2008, I flew to Quebec. When I arrived at the airport in Quebec, I looked for my luggage but I couldn't find it. I went to the police to file a claim with them. They investigated, but they couldn't find it either. I was very worried, because I had everything in my luggage. Jean-Yves and his wife came to the airport to pick me up, and after looking for it a second time, we decided to leave the airport.

When we arrived at their two-story house, they showed me where I would be sleeping. I also met their daughters. As soon as I saw Catherine

Jean-Yves daughter, I felt a connection with her; I was drawn to her deep black eyes and long, black hair. I really liked their house. In my dreams, I wanted myself to have one like it or even just live in Quebec. They made me feel very comfortable.

It was almost lunch time, so I went to help in the kitchen. Later, I set the table. We talked a lot about life in general. I regretted not having my luggage, because I had brought some gifts for them. After lunch, we decided to sit in the living room to admire the Christmas tree.

On my first night while I was trying to sleep, I suddenly felt like an energy was grabbing me on my arms. This energy wanted to be closer to me. I also felt heavy, long hair. Frightened, I rejected this energy that was insisting on getting closer to me. I prayed to God that I would not feel it anymore.

Around two thirty a.m., I opened my eyes again. This time, I saw some angel lights. Those lights were red, white, blue, and orange. Because I was half asleep, I didn't have the energy to get up and try to touch them.

The next morning while we were at the kitchen table for breakfast, I told the family what had happened to me the night before. Jean-Yves told me that Catherine had also seen this energy, which was actually a little blond girl. Catherine had some ability to see the future, and she confirmed for me what Jean-Yves had said.

Discovering My Identity
as an Indigo Adult

THE MORE I WENT TO AA, the more I got bored. I was tired of hearing others talk about their drinking problems. I wanted to understand things that some people weren't interested in, like "What are we here for?", "What is our purpose in life?", and especially "Who are we?" Slowly, I gave up on going to meetings because I wasn't learning anything.

Instead, I took the time to learn about myself by reading books and making myself aware of my deepest fears, joys, frustrations, and anger. That was how I discovered that I was an Indigo adult. Some characteristics of the Indigo include:

- unusual sensitivities,
- feelings of being misunderstood and separated from the real world,
- frustration and dissatisfactions with the world,
- very deep feelings and thoughts,
- introspection,
- a need to be in a better world, and
- a need for more out of life.

That was mostly how I felt; I still feel that way. I frequently went back and forth to and from my old ways. Being an Indigo isn't easy, because I discovered that people don't necessarily understand me. I have an unusual sensitivity that enables me to sense everything around me through smell, hearing, sight, and touch. These extra sensitivities with the five senses are my sixth sense.

During my time at Georges May, I sometimes wrote in my free time. My poems are unusual. Some of the poems are in my first book *Feelings of an Indigo's Heart*, which I finished March 19, 2010. I spent almost nine months writing that book.

Meeting Gregg Schroeder

I WANT TO TELL YOU that I have met the most precious man in my life. He has been there for me since August of 2010. His name is Gregg Schroeder. Even with my trust issues, I can tell you that he is someone I can count on. There are a lot of things I like about him. He gives me something that I have been missing my entire life, and that thing is love. I believe we are meant for each other.

This is the end of the first part of my story. I hope you liked it, and I wish you success in your life.

I am well aware of who I am now, and I want you to feel free to ask yourself the questions I have been asking myself:

"Who are you?"

"What is the purpose of your life?"

Here are a few words in French: *Ayez le courage d'être vous-même, même si vous devez vous faire des ennemies.* The meaning in English is: Have the courage to be yourself, even if you have to make enemies.